# the Oh Really? factor

# the Oh Really? factor

## Unspinning Fox News Channel's Bill O'Reilly

## PETER HART and
### Fairness & Accuracy in Reporting (FAIR)
### Foreword by Robert W. McChesney

seven stories press

New York | London | Toronto | Melbourne

Seven Stories Press
140 Watts Street
New York, NY 10013
www.sevenstories.com

In Canada: Hushion House, 36 Northline Road, Toronto, Ontario M4B 3E2

In the U.K: Turnaround Publisher Services Ltd., Unit 3,
Olympia Trading Estate, Coburg Road, Wood Green, London N22 6TZ

In Australia: Palgrave Macmillan, 627 Chapel Street, South Yarra VIC 3141

Library of Congress Cataloging-in-Publication Data

Hart, Peter, 1974-
  The oh really? factor : unspinning Fox News Channel's Bill O'Reilly /
by Peter Hart and Fairness and Accuracy in Reporting (FAIR).– 1st ed.
      p. cm.
  ISBN 1-58322-601-X (alk. paper)
  1. O'Reilly, Bill–Political and social views.  I. Fairness & Accuracy
in Reporting (Organization) II. Title.
PN4874.O73 H37 2003
791.45'02'8092–dc22                    2003015378

9  8  7  6  5  4  3  2  1

College professors may order examination copies of Seven Stories Press
titles for a free six-month trial period. To order, visit www.sevenstories.com/ textbook/,
or fax on school letterhead to (212) 226-1411.

Design by Cindy LaBreacht

Printed in Canada

# contents

5

# foreword
## The Golden Age of Irony

### by Robert W. McChesney

rony, my dictionary tells me, refers to "the use of words to express something the opposite of the literal meaning." In that case, we are in the Golden Age of Irony, and one need look no further than the Fox News Channel for confirmation. For years its slogans have been "We Report, You Decide" and "Fair and Balanced." But the Fox News Channel decides what to report and how to report it, so one's decision-making process is weighted by Fox's thumb on the scale. As for "fair and balanced," that all depends where one places the baseline. If one starts from the assumption that George W. Bush is at the center of the range of legitimate debate, and the further one gets from G. W. Bush, the more one's views must be "balanced," if not ignored altogether, the possibility of actually doing critical journalism toward those in power diminishes to the point of virtual nonexistence.

But the heavyweight champion of irony is no doubt Bill O'Reilly, whose *The O'Reilly Factor* is the network's most visible and successful program. Every program begins with O'Reilly's pronouncement that his show comprises a "no-spin zone" where all the B.S. and hot air that politicians and hustlers try to spew before the American people to mask their naked self-interest will be exposed for the tripe it is. O'Reilly claims to slice through the crap and reveal the truth to the masses. As one watches this lover of truth slay his victims on a nightly basis, one is to

7

be reminded of the plain-talking, straight-shooting classic American hero, a veritable Abe Lincoln from a Long Island log cabin.

It is Peter Hart's service that he shows us in detail just how preposterous O'Reilly's claim is to overseeing a "no-spin zone." Indeed, as Hart deftly demonstrates, O'Reilly is the ultimate spinmeister, the consummate propagandist. And as they teach in Propaganda 101, the first argument of the successful propagandist is to claim that what you are doing is telling the straight truth, while everyone with whom you disagree is doctoring their story to cover up their flaws. In O'Reilly's case, the "no-spin zone" is a place where most Republicans get treated with kid gloves, while their adversaries are raked over the coals. The double standard, as Hart reveals, is palpable. So it was that O'Reilly impaled Bill Clinton for the crime of lying about oral sex, while G. W. Bush is exonerated as he lies repeatedly to justify a preemptive attack and occupation of another country.

Those not especially familiar with *The O'Reilly Factor* may be surprised as they read this book and learn of O'Reilly's bullying tactics and self-obsession. These are the elements that have contributed to the show's success, and to the creation of the O'Reilly "brand." This is what makes the program entertaining and popular, and I share the attraction to shows about politics that feature argument and passion. But in O'Reilly's case, the contribution to our political culture comes at a high price. What struck me most, and should bring pause to everyone who reads this book, is the cavalier manner in which O'Reilly routinely lies, exaggerates, and misstates the truth. It is one thing to make misstatements on a daily TV program; that is going to happen periodically even under the best of circumstances. But O'Reilly does so repeatedly and shamelessly. O'Reilly's disinterest in the truth, in principle, in interrogating his own assumptions, and in intellectual consistency is little short of breathtaking.

How then do we reconcile the success of *The O'Reilly Factor* with its severe flaws as a public affairs program? There are two lessons that

8

jump out as one reads this book. First, to the handful of mega-corporations that rule the U.S. media system, journalism is a business and the bottom line rules. *The O'Reilly Factor* is perfect for corporate journalism. It costs almost nothing to produce as it is merely O'Reilly pontificating from this throne. It would appear that even a standard budget for research assistants and fact-checkers has been eliminated. So even though the program draws a fairly small audience in the broad scheme of U.S. television, through advertising it can generate large profits. Increasingly, it is clear that what makes for good journalism makes for bad profits, so we get bad journalism. O'Reilly is paid like a commercial entertainer and that is exactly what he is in the mind of Rupert Murdoch, whose News Corporation owns the Fox News Channel. That he fudges the truth is irrelevant—look at the money he is making! And from O'Reilly's perspective, he is making a fortune spewing out this stuff, so he must be doing something right. It is a depressing thought that more than a few Americans regard a nightly O'Reilly fix as their effort at keeping up with world events.

Second, what passes for political conservatism today in the United States is little more than crass opportunism wrapped in thousand-dollar bills. Peter Hart properly and graciously notes several times that there is nothing wrong with one adopting a conservative political position. I was raised in a proudly conservative household. But if Edmund Burke or Benjamin Disraeli or Robert Taft or even Barry Goldwater came back and saw what passes for conservatism today, they would, to take a line from the Woody Allen film *Hannah and Her Sisters*, never stop throwing up. Traditional concerns about big government and individual rights, a commitment to principle and integrity, a skepticism toward militarism, all of this has been tossed aside on *The O'Reilly Factor*. The only apparent principle is to help the G. W. Bush administration maintain power, and the overriding goal of the Bush administration is to shift as much of the resources of this nation into the hands of the wealthy as

quickly and thoroughly as possible. After that, all principle is shelved. The ends justify the means. And, oh yes, this is all being done on behalf of the "little guy." Irony reigns supreme.

Welcome to the world of O'Reilly, a striking measure of our dubious times.

# introduction
## The ALL-Spin Zone

**"Caution: You're about to enter a No-Spin Zone."**

With that warning, Fox News Channel's Bill O'Reilly kicks off *The O'Reilly Factor*, the most popular news show on cable television. Part interview, part commentary, the program is all O'Reilly. It's made him the object of both intense criticism and feverish praise. His books fly off the shelves, he writes a weekly newspaper column, and for anyone who can't get enough of him, there's now a syndicated *The Radio Factor with Bill O'Reilly* program on stations across the country. O'Reilly also appears on Fox's broadcast outlets, supplying commentary segments to Fox's newsmagazine *The Pulse* and producing one-hour specials, such as *The Corruption of the American Child*.

*Playboy* magazine aptly described O'Reilly as "the man who is simultaneously the most revered and most loathed on television these days." O'Reilly's fans see him as a tireless truth-seeker taking on the elites. Critics see a boorish, arrogant host who's never wrong.

"He's a made-for-television caricature who blows out bumper stickers," wrote Jim Wooten of the *Atlanta Journal-Constitution*. The *Minneapolis Star Tribune*'s Kristin Tillotson wrote that O'Reilly is "America's favorite carnival barker, with guests who disagree with him as his sideshow." CNN's Tucker Carlson once quipped, "Only masochists would go on his show—or watch it."

11

Everyone would probably agree on one thing: As the *Boston Globe* put it, "O'Reilly has managed to mold his don't-B.S.-me-and-the-folks persona into a brand of Nike proportions."

The O'Reilly "brand" is based on a simple marketing scheme: a straight-talking, working-class television show where the host cuts to the chase and demolishes the "spin" of his guests. In truth, it's an *all*-spin zone, where the host absurdly denies the show's conservative political slant and "facts" are manipulated in order to win arguments against O'Reilly's opponents.

## The "Pinhead" Factor

If you want a careful discussion of the news of the day, *The O'Reilly Factor* is probably the last place you should look. The show isn't about journalism per se; it more resembles a street fight, where guests who represent disagreeable ideas are called forth to be ridiculed or cut down. If you survive, you get points for "taking the fire" from O'Reilly.

Listen to O'Reilly describe the show in his words: Michael Kinsley criticized O'Reilly in print, but he "got murdered" (3/23/01) when he came on the show. Hip-hop mogul Russell Simmons wasn't just interviewed; "We slapped him around" is how O'Reilly described it (9/25/02). "We have nailed Jesse Jackson to the wall" is how he imagines his investigation into Jesse Jackson's finances, a never-ending saga on the show that is defined more by nastiness than by actual reporting. (Jackson has "never had a job" was one of O'Reilly's early insights.)

O'Reilly's most cherished insult is to call someone a "pinhead," an epithet he dispenses freely. When NBC's Matt Lauer interviewed O'Reilly about his drive to get the September 11 charities to distribute funds more quickly, Lauer had the audacity to suggest that such a massive undertaking could be expected to take some time. "You're being an apologist for pinheads," O'Reilly shot back.

# That's Your Opinion!

While the promise of *The O'Reilly Factor* is to make spinning guests sit still long enough to get the truth out of them, O'Reilly doesn't play by his own rules. Here is one of O'Reilly's favorite debating tactics: Faced with a factual statement he's unable to rebut, he accuses his guest of stating an opinion. When a journalist mentioned Israel's "illegal settlers" (7/18/00), O'Reilly replied, "All right, that's your opinion!" When a drug-policy advocate said marijuana impairs driving less than alcohol does (1/3/00), the answer was, "Well, that's your opinion!" When Greenpeace's John Passacantando asserted that drilling in the Arctic National Wildlife Refuge would only yield six to nine months of oil (5/1/01), O'Reilly was not impressed. "That's your opinion!" he retorted.

Faced with opinions—or facts—he doesn't care for, O'Reilly will interrupt only to make the point that a guest is just expressing an opinion (which is presumably the very reason they were invited on the show in the first place). When Kenneth Roth of Human Rights Watch noted that he sees the Bush administration "ripping up the Geneva Convention in Guantánamo," O'Reilly stopped him: "That's your opinion there. I mean that's not a fact, that's your opinion." Or O'Reilly will argue against a guest's opinion because it can't be proven. When David Corn of *The Nation* suggested that there could be alternatives to war with Iraq ("I'm saying there are alternatives to invasion and occupation"), O'Reilly huffed: "It's your opinion there is. You don't know that to be true."

O'Reilly, on the other hand, is free to dispense his own opinions or toss around unproven allegations. O'Reilly once asked a guest about Jesse Jackson using non-profit money to assist his out-of-wedlock daughter and her mother: "He could be, possibly, using it to stash the mistress for two years. Doesn't that upset you?" When the guest explained that there was no evidence that this was true, O'Reilly interjected, "Come on! Connect the dots!" (1/18/01)

To hear O'Reilly tell it, this kind of "candor" is a breath of fresh air in the timid TV news business. As he asked ABC's Peter Jennings, "Doesn't it drive you crazy that you know Arafat, you know these guys, yet you can't look into the camera and say, 'You know, that guy is a pinhead. He's doing the wrong thing. He should be doing this,' and you can't do that? Doesn't it drive you nuts?"

O'Reilly would like to see more journalists do what he does. Just imagine it: more reporters acting like Bill O'Reilly. But perhaps not quite every journalist should; O'Reilly is not at all impressed by former Clinton aide George Stephanopoulos's foray into journalism on ABC: "I don't believe a word he says. . . . I think he is an elitist snob who doesn't belong in the commentary realm at all." O'Reilly helpfully adds, "I wouldn't say take him off, I say I just can't stand him. And the reason is I think that his commentary is driven by an agenda."

If O'Reilly is turned off by anyone with an "agenda," it would sure seem odd for him to have settled at Rupert Murdoch's conservative Fox News Channel. But part of the agenda at Fox is to convince people they don't have one, and that's exactly what O'Reilly must do as well. Anyone who watches *The O'Reilly Factor*, however, can't help but notice that liberals and Democrats take a tremendous beating, while the GOP emerges relatively unscathed.

If you want to get O'Reilly angry, call him what he is—a conservative. The tilt in the show's story selection—to say nothing of O'Reilly's own opinions—was obvious to some TV critics from the start. Howard Rosenberg of the *Los Angeles Times* noticed that when *The O'Reilly Report* launched in 1996 (the "Factor" name came later), the lead guest was Billy Ray Dale, the former chief of the White House Travel Office. As Rosenberg wrote, "The interview was notable for its heavy-handed slant. Host Bill O'Reilly, a former *ABC News* correspondent and most recently anchor of the tabloid series *Inside Edition*, aggressively prodded Dale to bad-mouth Clinton and the first lady. When Dale said he hadn't paid

14

much notice of the first lady when he was in the audience of Sunday's Clinton-Dole debate in Hartford, Connecticut, O'Reilly was astonished. 'If I was you I would have turned around and stared at her,' O'Reilly said."

From that first day, very little has changed: Clinton scandals (of either the Bill or Hillary variety) still lurk, "political correctness" must be rooted out, and prominent liberal figures such as Jesse Jackson are demonized ("There are not two more exploitative people than Tim Robbins and Susan Sarandon," 4/11/03).

## Who Is Bill O'Reilly?

O'Reilly's fast rise to the top of the cable news game probably left some viewers wondering, "Who is this guy?" He might have looked vaguely familiar from his days as a network correspondent, but O'Reilly was perhaps best known as the host of the infotainment tabloid show *Inside Edition*.

O'Reilly bristles at the "tabloid" description and in the past has eagerly argued that since other network news divisions copied the style and presentation of *Inside Edition*, there was some credibility to what the show was doing. There's a very odd logic to the argument—if anything, it's proof that news standards at the networks were declining, but O'Reilly saw it the other way around.

There was one incident at *Inside Edition* that put the show even more at odds with the journalistic establishment. In 1994, the show paid professional skater Tonya Harding for an interview. Critics rightly called it checkbook journalism, but O'Reilly explained it differently: "Payment of sources has been going on for eons in broadcast journalism" (8/29/94). While other voices in the debate tried to point out that news outlets, as a rule, generally frown on paying for access, O'Reilly implausibly claimed that "there are times that *Inside Edition* has to pay for stories, as do the networks. We have the same exact standards as the networks do" (CNN, 2/17/94).

> **Everything is a spin on this program. There's nothing wrong with that. You do it with great style. You're sort of a Rush Limbaugh with perfume.**
>
> —Bishop John Shelby Spong on *The O'Reilly Factor*, 4/3/02

## No Angles

Covering the ballot recount in Florida was no picnic for O'Reilly. As he told the *Washington Post*, "You're trapped in a box full of numbers. With Monica Lewinsky, you could say, 'She's a tramp,' 'She's not a tramp.' You could do psychoanalysis. This is a one-dimensional story. You have to keep looking for new angles."

O'Reilly rates NBC anchor Katie Couric: "Katie Couric is interesting. I understand her appeal. As she gets older, she is much more attractive in every way. She has a dignity after surviving personal traumas. That's what I look for. That's sexy in a way we were never told about." (*Playboy*, 5/1/02; Couric's husband died in 1998)

## Reality TV?

On the influence of the actress Jennifer Aniston: "In my opinion, she is the most powerful female icon television has ever seen. Millions of young women imitate her look and find her extremely interesting. This season on her sitcom *Friends*, Ms. Aniston is having a child out of wedlock. . . . And she is planting a subliminal thing in an impressionable eight- and nine-year-old. Am I crazy here?"

"While serving as U.S. Attorney in Dade County, Ms. Reno presided over an area that had the worst drug importation problem in U.S. history. Remember *Miami Vice*? That was Janet Reno's turf. She saw it all firsthand. It was totally out of control, and that's kind of her background" (12/21/99).

O'Reilly's description of *Inside Edition* sounds remarkably similar to his description of *The O'Reilly Factor*: "We tap into the sensibilities of the middle class, the working class. It's fine to do stories about Bosnia, Romania, and South Africa, but what our viewers care most about is what is happening where they live, stories such as the one here in the Norfolk area about a convicted murderer who is allowed to walk away from a psychiatric hospital . . . We speak to the heartland of America" *(Norfolk Virginian-Pilot*, 5/3/94).

This is the approach he takes to *The O'Reilly Factor*, too. "The true measure of any TV program is the audience," O'Reilly once explained. You can't help but find that self-serving, given O'Reilly's place atop the cable ratings heap. But to judge one's work based on audience share is dangerous for a journalist. Good journalism—be it commentary or investigative reporting—rests on sound judgment, honesty, and accuracy. O'Reilly is winning the race to capture the largest audience, but that doesn't make what he does good journalism.

# No-Spin Zone?
## Don't Call O'Reilly Conservative—But He Is

From the top levels of its parent company, News Corporation, down to the on-air talent, there was a vision for Fox News Channel: a twenty-four-hour cable channel tailored to a conservative audience—folks who might want to watch TV that resembles the bare-knuckle style of right-wing talk radio. Yet the slogans of the network—"Fair and Balanced" and "We Report, You Decide"—imply that political skew is what infects its competitors. As its spokespeople are more than happy to explain, Fox is correcting for the media's left-wing tilt. The strategy might seem contradictory, but the ratings suggest that Fox has found its audience.

If News Corporation's head, Rupert Murdoch, needed a host who could embody this corporate vision—a high-decibel infotainer who could champion the channel's conservative politics, while at the same time denying them—he could probably do no better than Bill O'Reilly. He epitomizes Fox's in-your-face style, posing nightly as an outraged common man speaking out against the corruption of the liberal elites who run the country from the power centers of Hollywood and Washington. "We're the only show from a working-class point of view," he once told the *Washington Post* (12/13/00).

So is Bill O'Reilly a conservative? To anyone who watches his TV show, reads his opinion columns, or listens to his radio show, that probably sounds like a silly question. The obvious answer is yes.

There's nothing wrong with being a conservative, of course, just as there is no shame in being on the Left. This book, like other work by

19

FAIR, is informed by our own progressive politics. It's not that O'Reilly denies that he has opinions—they're what drive his show: "As I explained a gazillion times, this is a news analysis program which is driven by opinion. That is clearly labeled on your TV screen. I realize this is a departure from the bland traditional TV news, but the concept really isn't that difficult to get" (1/18/99).

What *is* difficult to "get" is how angry O'Reilly becomes when anyone tries to characterize his opinions. He goes out of his way to challenge anyone who wants to hang a political label on him. O'Reilly's strenuous denial that he's a right-winger is the first—and perhaps the biggest—lie about his show.

Despite assailing Hollywood liberals and Hillary Clinton night after night—he had an image of Hillary Clinton's face on his office doormat for quite some time—O'Reilly maintains that his views aren't conservative at all. He frequently proclaims his independence from all partisan agendas, as he wrote in his book *The O'Reilly Factor* (Broadway Books, 2000): "See, I don't want to fit any of those labels, because I believe that the truth doesn't have labels." The show's popular "No-Spin Zone" slogan is repeated ad nauseam by O'Reilly, as though it were prima facie evidence that the show is even-handed: "That's what the No-Spin Zone is all about: shooting down propaganda" (1/23/01).

"I'm not a conservative," O'Reilly once explained to a guest (5/4/01). "You think I'm a conservative?" he asked another. "See, that's a big misnomer" (8/10/01). Because the notion that his show is free of "spin" is so patently absurd, O'Reilly's critics lay into him for this political deception. In turn, O'Reilly angrily denies these accusations. Responding to critics in the hip-hop community—who find themselves frequent targets of O'Reilly's ire—he said their claim that he is right-wing "is ridiculous and absurd" (*New York Post*, 2/26/03).

There's almost a streak of paranoia to it; in one case, he invented a partisan accusation against him. Speaking about the *Boston Globe*,

O'Reilly lamented, "They called me today a conservative attack dog. That's their clever description of yours truly" (12/7/01). The paper actually just called him an "attack dog."

## O'Reilly's Enemies

O'Reilly's vehement denials come across as more than a little disingenuous, since his show is defined by his seemingly bottomless supply of anger, and it's no secret that O'Reilly has his favorite targets: Democratic politicians (Ted Kennedy, Bill and Hillary Clinton, Tom Daschle), public figures associated with liberal causes (Jesse Jackson, Hollywood stars such as Barbra Streisand), and hot-button political issues that he can use to bash the Left (anything from reparations for slavery to "political correctness"). Notice a pattern here?

> **"There is no question that Mrs. Clinton is the most controversial person in the world today."** (6/22/00)

Groups or individuals critical of the George W. Bush administration are scorned: the American Civil Liberties Union (ACLU) is labeled a "fascist" organization because of its criticisms of civil liberties infringements in the wake of September 11 (not to mention its steadfast belief in the separation of church and state): "The ACLU has now become a fascist organization that is imposing a perverted interpretation of the Constitution upon the American people." Amnesty International's criticism of White House policy earns a swift rebuke: "I've pretty much had it with Amnesty International" (5/29/02).

When not attacking Bush's critics, O'Reilly's nightly program gives him a platform to whack the opposition party. His description of the Democratic Party could have been lifted right from the script of Rush Limbaugh or Fox cohort Sean Hannity—consider this "question" to former Clinton press secretary Dee Dee Myers: "What else besides taxing working Americans and building up big entitlement programs do you guys stand for? Is there anything else that you stand for?" (11/6/02) O'Reilly backed a congressional investigation into the September 11 attacks, with one caveat:

that Democratic Senator Tom Daschle be excluded, as "he has a major axe to grind and is a champion of partisan bickering . . . So with all due respect, senator, shut up." (And O'Reilly wonders why Daschle won't come on his show!) While some considered it off-limits to discuss government policy as a cause of the September 11 attacks, O'Reilly was an exception, as long as it offered him a free shot at one of his enemies: "The Clinton administration thought they could contain bin Laden. The result of that policy [is] three thousand Americans dead" (8/9/02).

The evidence of O'Reilly's conservatism is not just his targets, though. The tone of O'Reilly's attacks reveals his ideological commitments loud and clear:

 **Nobody should begrudge any American the right to an opinion, but, hey, Rosie [O'Donnell], come on, let's think out your flaky liberal agenda a little. Are you making sense, or are you spouting propaganda? I mean, a guy named Joseph Goebbels did the same thing on the far right during World War II.** (*The O'Reilly Factor*, p. 184)

**I've never seen a colder, more calculating politician in this country than Hillary Clinton.** *(Playboy* interview, 5/1/02)

O'Reilly can spin all day about his supposed independence, but the evidence on the screen every night says otherwise. From the "Talking Points" commentaries that open the show to the skew in the story selection, the evidence overwhelmingly undermines his argument. On most nights it's not hard to tell where the show is headed right from the opening bell:

**TONIGHT: Why do some countries like France want to keep the vicious dictator Saddam Hussein in power? We will tell**

you. Former weapons inspectors and antiwar guy Scott Ritter is accused of seeking sex with a fourteen-year-old. Is his credibility shot? Your tax dollars at work: Rap is being taught in some public schools. We'll find out why. And the truth about race in the military. (1/21/03)

TONIGHT: Violent demonstrations on the rise all over the world as capitalism comes under assault and America's college campuses are being besieged with socialistic messages. We'll have a report. The first hundred days of Hillary Clinton in the Senate. Did she actually do anything? We'll find out. And was Al Gore antagonistic toward some of his students at Columbia? That's the word. (5/2/01)

Oddly enough, after that kind of introduction, the next words out of O'Reilly's mouth are this familiar warning: "Caution: You're about to enter a No-Spin Zone."

His newspaper columns and two best-selling books are much the same. "It is becoming very hard for independent thinkers to embrace the American Left these days," began one of his commentaries in the *Washington Times* (1/2/02). What had the Left done now? "Over the holiday season, we were barraged with articles and TV news spots about the growing legion of homeless Americans—stories that were designed to make us feel guilty." O'Reilly's frequent digs at the Left are the red meat that is served up for a conservative audience: "The terrorists love Berkeley, California, because many in that town 'see no evil,' no matter how brutal the situation" (*Washington Times*, 10/23/01). A supposedly "independent" thinker might be expected to direct similar fire at the Right, but in O'Reilly's world that almost never happens.

The drive to disparage his political opponents can lead to some remarkable hypocrisy. O'Reilly devoted one segment (2/18/03) to exposing the Ford Foundation for its financial support of immigrant rights groups, saying to his guest, "The Ford Foundation, which is a giant philanthropic group, all right, has given, in the past thirty years, $57 million to five groups that don't want a crackdown on the border. Is that true?" That guest, Dan Stein of the Federation for American Immigration Reform, filled in the details for O'Reilly. But O'Reilly's viewers (and presumably his staff) were unaware of details of sources of Stein's own funding: his group has received support from the Pioneer Fund, a foundation that advocates the racist pseudoscience of eugenics.

O'Reilly's tendency to direct most of his fire at liberals —or anyone to his left—hasn't gone unnoticed. On one segment (3/7/01) dedicated to O'Reilly's endless "investigation" into Jesse Jackson, guest Steve Sherman wondered if O'Reilly had the same interest in conservative nonprofits: "I don't see you asking for the disclosure of their finances." O'Reilly replied, "Sure I do. If they have a tax-exempt status we watch them. We just did a report on the Morris Dees organization down in Alabama. Anybody that comes across our viewfinder that's not playing by the rules, we're going to report on." But the group "down in Alabama" is the Southern Poverty Law Center, which monitors racist organizations and the far Right—not exactly a conservative group.

> One *Factor* guest gets right to the point: "When I agree with you, I'm reasoning. And when I have a different point of view, then I'm being unreasonable. That's no spin. That's the No-Spin Zone" (1/20/03).

## No Spin?

So what else makes Bill O'Reilly a conservative? For starters, it's difficult to find many policy decisions by the Bush administration that he hasn't supported. When there is disagreement, he offers only the mildest criticisms—and often from the administration's right (on issues such as immigration, where he favors placing the military at the borders, or their

unwillingness to sufficiently investigate Clinton-era shenanigans). He was among the strongest supporters of Bush's tax-cut proposals, which were tilted heavily toward the wealthy—himself included. Guests who dared to point out that plain fact were accused of dishonesty: "Oh, that's propaganda. You know nobody buys that. Are you going to still do that? Tax cuts to the wealthy? Are you going to still bang that mantra? Nobody buys that stuff" (interview with Al Sharpton, 11/7/02).

But that's just the start.

## ABORTION

O'Reilly thinks there are pro-choice "forces of darkness" that pose a threat to America:

**If you don't believe the American family is under siege by some very powerful forces, please continue reading. The American Civil Liberties Union, Planned Parenthood, and some powerful politicians—most notably Hillary Clinton—are on a jihad to pass laws allowing underage girls to have abortions without parental consent. (*Washington Times*, 9/10/01)**

**No matter what you believe about abortion, this much is true in America: we are now a country that has devalued the lives of infants, and a good case can be made that the widespread acceptance of abortion has led to that. (6/30/99)**

## FEMINISM

**The National Organization for Women and other feminist groups do not want to give men any power. They want to take power away from men. (3/4/02)**

O'Reilly reportedly called the president of the National Organization for Women a "loon" in a speech (*Ventura [Calif.] County Star*, 2/13/02).

## PRIVATIZE IT!

"The government should get out of the service business so politicians can't buy union votes," says O'Reilly. He advocates the privatization of "Amtrak, subway and bus systems, road maintenance, garbage collection, most other services, exclusive of police and fire" (12/9/02).

He supports privatization of Social Security, though his interest in it seems oddly pegged to bashing his favorite target, Jesse Jackson: "But the actual money that they take out of the Social Security fund flows right into the general fund, and it's spent on Jesse Jackson's tax-exempt organizations and everything like that, right?" (3/8/01)

## LABOR UNIONS

For a supposedly working-class guy, O'Reilly certainly has little good to say about labor unions: "When you land after a five-hour trans-con flight and have to sit on the runway for another hour because the union guys are on a break and no gate is available, that's simply unacceptable" (8/13/02).

"So it comes back to the unions, doesn't it? Isn't this the problem in America's public schools—the unions?" O'Reilly answered his own question: "The unions don't care about these children. They care about their power base. And the Democratic Party doesn't care about those poor children. They care about getting the money and the votes from the unions. And it's a disgrace, and that's the bottom line here" (1/23/01).

## HOMELESSNESS

I don't want my children, after working hard and buying a house in a beautiful neighborhood, being exposed to bizarre behavior. I don't believe those people, these homeless, have a right to that bizarre behavior. And sleeping in a doorway when it's twenty degrees is bizarre behavior. (12/19/02)

## MISSILE DEFENSE

When an American spy plane went down in China, it inexplicably provided proof that the United States needs a "Star Wars" missile defense system: "That very expensive missile shield President Bush wants to build is now a lock. After seeing how the Chinese behaved in this incident, we need a shield" (4/12/01).

## GOING NUCLEAR

**Nuclear power is not an option anymore—it's a must. (5/17/01)**

## GOING AFTER SECULARISM

"I am the only commentator on television at this point that routinely attacks the secularists," O'Reilly once boasted (1/15/03). That position makes O'Reilly a lonely voice in the media, as "there is no question that a secular agenda is in play in many newsrooms. . . . If the papers or the TV networks' view is that secularism is best for America, they have a right to that opinion, even if I think it's misguided and destructive to the country. And I do, because we have few moral boundaries left in America. You can pin that directly on secularism."

## O'REILLY THE HAWK

There's hardly an American military campaign that O'Reilly has not backed to the fullest, especially the U.S. war in Iraq. Critics of Bush's Iraq policy were advised to "shut up" once war began and were derided as un-American. (O'Reilly was eventually troubled by this designation and switched to

the evidently less problematic "bad Americans.") He also supports the economic embargo against Cuba: "If you liberalize your policy toward Cuba, then you reward Fidel Castro for his just intolerable regime" (4/28/00).

## PRAYER IN SCHOOL

 **When there was school prayer and when there was an emphasis on God—"one nation under God"—in the schools, there was a morality that went along with that: Thou shalt not kill, thou shalt not hurt your neighbor. Now that's all gone and, to me, I don't think that's a good thing. (4/28/99)**

## DRUG TESTING THE POOR

"I think you have to drug test everybody on welfare" (3/30/00). O'Reilly expressed outrage after the Supreme Court ruled that a program in South Carolina to test all maternity patients was unconstitutional: "Drug-addicted pregnant women no longer have anything to fear from the authorities thanks to the Supreme Court" (3/23/01).

## SOCIAL SPENDING

"I'm not real keen on handing over any more dough to a system that will not even drugtest Americans receiving entitlement checks in the mail." For a man of the people, O'Reilly could hardly express more contempt for the disadvantaged: "It is a myth that people cannot get jobs. There are plenty of jobs available almost everywhere" (4/9/01).

O'Reilly prefaced a question to one guest by making the Reaganesque point that "my opinion is that most people who are poor in America are poor because they want to be poor, because they're substance abusers or they do something irresponsible," adding that "I don't believe that my money and everybody's money who's worked for a living should be

going to people who are on crack. I don't believe that. Yet it continues and continues into the trillions of entitlement money that goes right down the rat hole" (4/19/01).

## ALL HAIL REAGANOMICS

O'Reilly's stance on economics is unmistakably right-wing: "Well, look, you can laugh at trickle-down economics, but it's worked for a hundred years here in the United States." And O'Reilly advises us to thank Ronald Reagan for the boom of the 1990s: "Reagan ran huge deficits, and then in the nineties it all whiptailed into a great economy" (1/29/03).

## O'REILLY'S MORAL RECTITUDE

O'Reilly also spews outrage over America's supposed moral decline, whether it's public funding for "offensive" art or rap music (lecturing the editor of hip-hop magazine *The Source* on 2/18/03: "You sell mind poison. You've gotten rich off that . . . just like a drug dealer, OK").

The most insignificant breaches of O'Reilly's puritanical social values are discussed at length: A pornographic film is shot in a dorm room at Indiana University, and O'Reilly devotes segment after segment to shredding the students and administrators for their behavior; the local media, meanwhile, get a drubbing for not matching his level of outrage. One might think high school students caught having sex on a school bus in Massachusetts isn't a story worth much media attention, but O'Reilly elevates the incident to a national scandal, devoting several segments to the tale, as it provides ample evidence of the erosion of appropriate discipline in the public schools.

O'Reilly's social conservatism blends nicely with his political beliefs. As O'Reilly wrote in his second book, *The No Spin Zone* (Broadway Books, 2001), Bill Clinton's personal behavior had some unintended conse-

### HIP-HOP=AL QAEDA?

"Eminem may be the 'people's choice,' but, in reality, he is as harmful to America as any al Qaeda fanatic." (*Ventura* [Calif.] *County Star*, 1/18/03)

29

quences: "The president himself set a terrific example by lying outright to the nation on national television. None of this, of course, was lost on the kids, who, according to a variety of surveys, are lying like crazy and have now embraced oral sex with, you might say, presidential abandon."

## Getting Active

Until recently, O'Reilly was content to vent his spleen about these matters and leave it at that. But of late, he has openly advocated boycotts, as well as government or legal action, to support his crusades. When he discovered that the VH1 cable channel was going to air *Music Behind Bars*, a show about musical programs for prison inmates, O'Reilly pledged to fund a class action against VH1's parent company, Viacom, on behalf of the victims' families, who O'Reilly maintained were traumatized by seeing those who had committed crimes against their family members. (An ironic side note: O'Reilly's radio show is syndicated by Westwood One, a company run by Viacom's Infinity Radio division.)

During singer Whitney Houston's confessional interview on ABC's *Primetime Live* with Diane Sawyer (12/4/02), her acknowledgment that she used drugs seemed to enrage O'Reilly. He did a few segments about Houston's drug use after the interview aired and eventually called the authorities in New Jersey, where Houston lives, to report her for child abuse: "We're the only program that's explored this, the only people that have called or done anything or asked questions about the social services. Nobody else has done it." O'Reilly was realistic about the outcome: "I don't expect anything will happen, but we have made the calls" (12/9/02).

O'Reilly's sizeable audience has been encouraged to get in on the action, too. After Pepsi-Cola announced that rapper Ludacris would appear in a commercial for the soda, O'Reilly urged action against the company, arguing that the rapper's graphic lyrics should not be rewarded: "I'm calling for all Americans to say, 'Hey, Pepsi, I'm not drinking your stuff. You want to hang around with Ludacris, you do that; I'm not hanging around with you'" (8/27/02). Perhaps inspired by the "success" of this action—Pepsi quickly capitulated and dropped the sponsorship plan—O'Reilly moved on to a boycott of French products, due to that country's refusal to support the U.S. rush to war in Iraq. The boycott was inspired by an Internet poll at www.billoreilly.com, whose readers (here's a shock!) overwhelmingly supported the idea.

In fact, the "Contact Center" at www.billoreilly.com is a great place to get a sense of just who and what gets O'Reilly's goat. On a recent visit,

# O'Reilly's Appeal

Despite all the bluster about his political independence, O'Reilly has acknowledged that his core audience consists of "moderate conservatives" (*Washington Post*, 12/13/00). He was a featured columnist on the conservative website www.worldnet daily.com and his columns now appear at www.billoreilly.com. O'Reilly's appeal to conservatives extends to the highest levels of the Republican Party: He was even ushered in for a private meeting with George and Barbara Bush during the 2001 inauguration festivities (*Newsweek*, 2/12/01). Around the time of the GOP convention that year, O'Reilly gave the keynote speech at David Horowitz's conservative "Restoration Weekend" event, described by the *Washington Times* as the "premier political event for conservative thinkers" (6/30/00).

As it's unlikely that conservatives just love O'Reilly for his social grace, there must be something about his politics that appeals to the right. "What I do on television is what they do on the op-ed page of the newspapers, OK? That's what I do. I'm a columnist, kind of." And that's all true: *The O'Reilly Factor* is like the op-ed page of a conservative newspaper, with a conservative owner and a lead columnist who is conservative on most major issues.

# O'Reilly for Congress?

O'Reilly's "independent" cover was dealt a blow by a report in the *New York Daily News:* Despite his claims of being politically independent, O'Reilly had been a registered Republican in Nassau County since 1994 (12/6/00). The *Daily News* reported that O'Reilly was "clearly rattled" when informed of his party registration and quickly had it changed. O'Reilly later told *Washington Post* reporter Paul Farhi that the matter was simply a "clerical mistake."

That might be believable, but other facts raise questions. On two different occasions, O'Reilly has been considered a strong candidate for Congress—as a Republican. According to a report in the *Boston Globe* (10/24/89), O'Reilly was an attractive option for the GOP in their drive to unseat liberal Democratic Congressman Barney Frank. The paper reported that O'Reilly was "mulling a run against Frank on the Republican ticket" and was scheduled to meet with Bush White House aide Ron Kaufman about a run. At the time, O'Reilly lived in New Jersey and was anchoring *Inside Edition*. Five years later, when he announced that he was leaving that program, the "O'Reilly for Congress" idea resurfaced. According to a report about his life after *Inside Edition*, O'Reilly "named a number of future options, including a possible run for Congress, likely as a Republican" (*Daily Variety*, 10/17/04). The *Hollywood Reporter* noted that O'Reilly "said he had been asked by the Republican National Committee to run for Congress in 1996. 'I may be looking to do that,' he said" (10/17/94). The story had apparently been floating around for a few months; *Newsday* (2/14/94) claimed that O'Reilly "has his eye on a Nassau County seat as a Republican," citing an item from *Esquire* magazine. O'Reilly told *Newsday*, "All the Republican guys are pretty well set, so I'm not going to go in against an incumbent." For the record, he envisioned campaigning on an anticrime platform that would include allowing the military to "take over some of the prison responsibilities so that the hard-core [criminals] will be taken out of our society where they can't hurt anyone; local and state systems can't handle it."

you could send an e-mail thanking British Prime Minister Tony Blair for supporting the war in Iraq, learn to avoid buying French products, or write an e-mail to the antiwar group Not In Our Name to "express your outrage" about their "claim the U.S. Government has 'declared a war without limit' and 'instituted stark new measures of repression.'"

## So Why All the Spinning?

That's quite a record for a guy who professes to have no particular political slant. His unmistakably ideological approach might not be entirely an accident; if anything, it appears to have been a deft career move. According to one report, O'Reilly found career inspiration in right-wing radio host Rush Limbaugh, telling one former colleague, "I'm not sure where the business is going, but my gut says it's going in the direction of Rush, and man, I'm going to be there" (*Boston Globe*, 12/1/02).

O'Reilly's conservatism does differ from Limbaugh's. For starters, O'Reilly regularly presents opposing viewpoints on his show, because part of the appeal is watching O'Reilly "destroy" guests who oppose him. He's also not nearly the political conformist that Limbaugh is, as he's more likely to express ideas that challenge conservative orthodoxy.

But it's hardly unusual for conservative TV pundits to have a few outlying views, so why all the spinning about his politics? Here are two major reasons why O'Reilly is forced to deny he's a conservative. First, admitting his point of view would destroy the show's marketing gimmick of being TV's "No-Spin Zone," an oasis of straight talk where slick ideologues are held to account.

Second and perhaps more importantly, it would make it much harder for Fox to maintain that the network's lineup doesn't lean right, because O'Reilly is packaged as an equal-opportunity gadfly, a populist who rails indiscriminately at the Left and the Right. When Fox News chief Roger Ailes told the *Washington Post* that "our prime time is just down the

middle," he cited as evidence the fact that O'Reilly "hammers everyone" (2/5/01). In practice, of course, it's almost always liberals and their friends who get hammered. Considering O'Reilly's very selective outrage, his heavy-handed moralizing, and his social conservatism, it's difficult to imagine that anyone buys his peculiar self-definition.

Yet some of his media colleagues do. ABC's Peter Jennings followed Roger Ailes's lead, calling O'Reilly "an equal-opportunity provocateur" (*People*, 12/18/00). Others don't buy O'Reilly's spin-free rhetoric. A *Boston Globe* profile sized him up more accurately: "Taken together, his views are overwhelmingly conservative. It's hard to see how a true populist can favor the permanent elimination of the estate tax, a burden imposed solely on the wealthiest 2 percent of the nation, [Rupert] Murdoch and O'Reilly among them" (12/1/02). Former Clinton Secretary of Labor Robert Reich also has little trouble seeing through O'Reilly's smoke screen. Reich pinned O'Reilly as "an obvious conservative Republican. But he can't say [so] on the air. . . . He can't have his perch and be an avowed conservative Republican."

## O'Reilly's Liberalism ("I Believe in Global Warming!")

O'Reilly and his Fox bosses seem aware of the need to mask the partisanship of their number-one show. When O'Reilly's claims of ideological neutrality are challenged, he reverts to a familiar script. As part of his "no-spin" marketing strategy, he has cultivated a handful of pet "liberal" political positions that he can rattle off when accused of being a conservative. But when O'Reilly actually expounds his "liberal" views, they often turn out to be conservative views in disguise.

For example, O'Reilly often touts himself as a staunch environmentalist to prove his ideological evenhandedness. But then he rails that "the greens have strangled the California economy" (5/10/01) and that envi-

ronmentalists are "distorting and oversimplifying some very powerful issues" (5/1/01). His concern for the environment isn't exactly deep; consider his reasons for supporting oil drilling in Alaska's Arctic National Wildlife Refuge: "I would drill in ANWR myself, just to see what's up there" (12/31/01).

O'Reilly's "liberal" stance on climate change is so qualified as to be practically a nonposition: "I believe there is global warming. I mean, I know that's controversial. For every scientist who says there is, there's one that says there isn't" (3/29/01). His convictions on the issue aren't exactly solid: "I can line up ten experts who will swear global warming is a threat to the world. And then I can get ten others who say, 'Hey, the whole thing is bogus. There's no global warming.' Since I haven't visited the ozone layer lately, I don't have a clue" (1/23/01). But while he may not understand climate science, he is keenly aware of the ideological value of his nonposition: "I'm not right-wing. I believe in global warming" (6/25/02). For O'Reilly, it's not really a principle; it's a way to disarm critics on both sides.

Similarly, his oft-proclaimed opposition to the death penalty quickly wanders off to the far right. O'Reilly's proposed substitute for capital punishment: Offenders "should all be subjected to life in prison without parole in a federal work camp" that "would be run military style and be located on federal land in Alaska. It would be in effect a gulag." Convicts would be "forced to labor eight hours a day, six days a week, in the harsh climate" and "if the criminal did not cooperate with the work detail, his food rations would be cut, and he would be placed in solitary confinement" (www.worldnetdaily.com column, 6/14/01).

He makes some exceptions to his objections to capital punishment—for public hangings. Consider this comment about poet Allen Ginsberg, who died in 1997: "I would have hung this guy Ginsberg if I could get my hands on him for all the damage he did to children" (9/30/02). O'Reilly seemed to refer to Ginsberg's ties to the North American Man/Boy Love Association, which perhaps in O'Reilly's world might merit execution.

But Ginsberg wasn't the only one: "How can any human being not condemn Gary Condit? It's ridiculous. We should hang him from the Capitol Building right now. I mean, this is a despicable human being. A guy who lied to a family in torment, a family in pain. This guy's a disgrace" (*Fox News Sunday*, 8/5/01).

One of O'Reilly's other "liberal" positions is his support of campaign finance reform. Again, it comes with a conservative spin: "I am for the McCain-Feingold bill with one big 'if.' They have to come up with limitations of union donations directly to candidates, hard money stuff, because unions can put pressure on their people to donate to candidates they don't even like" (3/22/01).

So next time you hear O'Reilly recite his "liberal" script, you might ask for the footnotes.

## Soft on Bush

O'Reilly has not hidden his fondness for George W. Bush. For a commentator who scrutinized virtually every action of the previous administration (letting up ever so slightly once Clinton was out of the White House), O'Reilly's soft treatment of the Bush administration speaks volumes: "President Bush ran on the slogan 'reformer with results.' That sounds good to me" (2/15/01), he cheered during Bush's first weeks in office. The praise and support don't end there. "For me, it's more comfortable with a guy like Bush," O'Reilly once explained (5/6/02). That's an understatement when you consider a comment like this: "I'll submit to you that George W. Bush is the closest modern president to what the Founding Fathers had in mind" (2/19/03).

O'Reilly is quick to jump to the defense of virtually every major initiative of the Bush White House—from the environment to missile defense—by laying into Bush's critics. When Bush won Senate passage of his tax cut plan, O'Reilly belittled its opponents: "How on earth could

thirty-eight Democratic senators vote against it? . . . This is not a big tax cut. . . . A tax cut that puts money in the pockets of all working Americans is a good thing, period" (5/24/01). That's anything but a "no-spin" interpretation of Bush's tax cut. But O'Reilly wanted more from Bush: "His tax cuts are too small to turn the markets around and he has inherited a mess from Mr. Clinton" (3/12/01).

When Bush appointed Dick Cheney to formulate the administration's energy policy, O'Reilly judged the former oilman a sound choice: "I would rather have a Cheney—even though I might disagree with him

## Commitment to Democracy?
## O'Reilly on the Florida Election Fiasco

The process is being abused and manipulated by people who will not accept the verdict in the state of Florida as it was put forth by machines. (12/1/00)

Look, we don't need this recount because the machines are nonbiased. What they threw out, they threw out. There was no machine malfunction. That was my take here, and I believe that stands today. (5/8/01)

He [George W. Bush] should look into any voting irregularities because the NAACP has filed suit, as you know, and he should also investigate Jesse Jackson's tax returns, and that would be even, and I think that would—I'd like to know both right there. I'd like to know both. (2/1/01)

BOB FERTIK (of www.democrats.com): "I believe in America every vote should count."

BILL O'REILLY: "Live with it. All right. With all due respect, every time you go back on that, anybody who's in the middle, not a Republican or a Democrat, thinks you're a geek. It's over, move on" (9/25/02).

sometimes—at least trying to do something than the hypocrites we had in [the] Clinton-Gore administration" (5/1/01).

Bush's deceptions haven't gotten him into hot water with O'Reilly. When Bush sought to de-emphasize his relationship with Enron CEO Kenneth Lay, he dissembled so badly that much of the media couldn't help but take notice. On January 10, 2001, he claimed that Lay "was a supporter of [Democratic Texas Governor] Ann Richards in my run in 1994. . . . And she did name him the head of the Governor's Business Council, and I decided to leave him in place just for the sake of continuity. And that's when I first got to know Ken and worked with Ken, and he supported my candidacy." In fact, according to Texans for Public Justice, Richards received $12,500 from Enron sources during the 1994 election cycle, while Bush got $146,500, including $47,500 from Lay and his wife, Linda. But this barely registered on the outrage meter of O'Reilly, who charitably noted that Bush "didn't lie. . . . He kind of, like, spun" (2/7/02).

On another episode of the *Factor* (12/16/02), guest Paul Loeb wondered why Bush got away with his false claim that an International Atomic Energy Agency report concluded that Iraq was mere months away from developing a nuclear weapon. In reality, no such report existed, and Loeb suggested that the president should be held accountable for his deception. But O'Reilly wasn't going to be the one to demand that Bush tell the truth: "Well, you could make that argument. And that's the argument that the electorate has to make . . . The American people have to make that argument and that decision." Why would a journalist so committed to pontificating about rights and wrongs in public life suddenly pull back from offering his opinion?

One example perhaps best sums up O'Reilly's kid gloves approach to the Bush White House. When O'Reilly was a guest on NPR's *Talk of the Nation* (7/30/02), a caller wondered why the legal watchdog group Judicial Watch, a fixture on the Fox News Channel when it was criticizing the

Clinton administration, was relatively absent now that it was criticizing the Bush White House. O'Reilly explained his notion of journalistic fairness this way:

 **It's hard to give a balanced report when the other side is unavailable. So you can say, for example, that Vice President Cheney—who I actually criticized this week on the Fox *Pulse* broadcast on Thursday night—you can say, "Oh, when he was at Halliburton, he did X, Y, and Z." Well, how do I know? I'm not there. I mean, I don't know what he did and what he didn't do. Now Judicial Watch can go fire fifteen guns at him, but I know I'm not going to get Cheney on to back it up, so it's almost irresponsible for me to just put on one side. That's what I've got to watch.**

Excuse me? A man who has made his reputation by slamming Jesse Jackson and the Clintons, often without a guest on hand who might challenge his claims, is able to say with a straight face that it would be unfair to subject the Bush administration to similar scrutiny. Case closed.

## Republicans Ride for Free in the No-Spin Zone

You can't argue that O'Reilly *never* criticizes Republicans. GOP heavyweights such as Attorney General John Ashcroft and Congressman Tom DeLay won't appear on the show because of criticisms O'Reilly has made of them on the air. Like O'Reilly's fallback "liberal" positions, he cites Ashcroft and DeLay when he needs to shore up his no-spin credentials. On its face, the argument might sound convincing: he must be tough because *both* sides dislike him, right?

But O'Reilly's criticisms of Republicans are often just a roundabout way of pounding Democrats. For example, O'Reilly's real beef with

Ashcroft is not that he's infringing on our civil liberties. O'Reilly's angry that Ashcroft won't investigate the Clinton pardons to his satisfaction: "If Ashcroft would do his job and investigate the Marc Rich pardon, Clinton would be in cuffs. That's bribery. But he won't" (1/23/03).

While politely disagreeing with Republican Senator Rick Santorum's equation of homosexuality with incest and bestiality, O'Reilly saved his real anger for Santorum's critics: "He can say whatever he wants about a legal matter now being heard by the Supreme Court, and the witch-hunters can stuff it. . . . If Santorum feels homosexual activity is wrong, he's entitled to that belief without being labeled a hater. The real haters are the witch-hunters, and we are watching them very closely" (4/23/03).

During the confirmation hearings for Attorney General John Ashcroft, critics of the nomination pointed out that as attorney general of Missouri, Ashcroft opposed a voluntary school desegregation plan. While O'Reilly did make an occasional criticism of Ashcroft's record here or there, he expended far more energy pounding Ashcroft's liberal opponents. They were using "cheap McCarthyistic tactics," and O'Reilly characterized the hearings as almost a ritual humiliation: "Did he have to be attacked, John Ashcroft? Did he have to be attacked by Ted Kennedy?" (1/19/01) A few nights earlier, O'Reilly made excuses for Ashcroft's position, saying "it was not a racial issue—it was a states' rights issue."

Even when O'Reilly had something critical to say about Ashcroft, there was a catch. Thus O'Reilly said that Ashcroft's "opposition to voluntary integration measures have to be illuminated. If I were an African American I'd be very concerned about John Ashcroft as attorney general." But then O'Reilly switched to a more familiar tactic: "But I would give him a chance to explain himself, and that's more than Barbara Boxer, Jesse Jackson, and other leftist ideologues will do. The only acceptable candidates to them are those who embrace their point of view or are afraid of them" (1/15/01). As usual, what begins as a critique of a conservative turns out to be a feint before the attack against O'Reilly's real targets.

Senator Trent Lott's tribute to retiring Senator Strom Thurmond was a case where a Republican took what most would consider an indefensible position. At a retirement celebration for Thurmond in December 2002, Lott said he was proud that the voters of Mississippi supported Thurmond's run for president in 1948, adding that "if the rest of the country had followed our lead, we wouldn't have had all these problems over all these years, either." Thurmond had run as a pro-segregation Dixiecrat. Soon after Lott made his comments, he was forced out as Senate majority leader.

Like the rest of the cable news world, O'Reilly was compelled to cover the story, but in his own inimitable way: "I'm tired of this story. At this point, the good people of Mississippi and the Republican senators have to deal with Lott. I don't, thank God" (12/17/02). To O'Reilly, the story of Lott's racism was "hot in the nation's capital. But outside the Beltway, much of the country is tired of hearing about it." Far from drawing any conclusions about Lott, O'Reilly preferred to leave that to the viewers. "It's up to you, the individual American, to form an opinion about Mr. Lott . . . at this point it is overkill to continue smashing the man." O'Reilly perplexingly added that, "If I were black, I'd be hoping he'd stick around" (12/17/02).

O'Reilly was even quick to grope for a distraction from Lott's racist "predicament." As he reported, "Last month vicious racial graffiti was painted on an African-American dormitory room at the University of Mississippi, Ole Miss, Lott's alma mater. At first authorities suspected white racists, but it turns out three black freshmen did the ugly deed, perhaps to provoke racial hatred" (12/18/02).

That strategy was similar to the one O'Reilly had used three years earlier, when Lott's connection to the racist Council of Conservative Citizens emerged. O'Reilly acknowledged and criticized Lott's connection to the group, but in the midst of the controversy found the time to investigate how "on the other hand, there is a group called the Congressional Progressive Caucus that some consider far left" (2/4/99). The Caucus

aroused O'Reilly's suspicion because it is "a bit socialist, I have to say."

The following night O'Reilly denied that he was trying to draw a comparison between a racist organization and a group of lefty lawmakers. O'Reilly's tease for the interview, however, suggests that a comparison was exactly what he was going for: "Coming next, Bob Barr and Trent Lott took heat for speaking to a far right group, but did you know that some congresspeople belong to a group that is very left?"

## Skewering Both Sides?

Even when O'Reilly self-consciously promises to skewer both sides, he fails to deliver. At the top of one commentary during the California energy crisis, O'Reilly promised "some straight talk about how our leaders on both sides have let us down once again, this time on the energy situation" (5/17/01). He began with a litany of complaints about the Clinton administration, which "knew more than two years ago that oil and gas prices were going to rocket because OPEC decided to cut production." Clinton "did not warn Americans" about this; he "also knew that California was running out of electricity but again kept silent, allowing that state to plunge into chaos. Inexplicably, the Clinton administration allowed California to be price-gouged by out-of-state power companies."

And what about the other side—what were the Republican failures? Well, Bush "is in no hurry to help California because that state is solidly against his policies, and the energy situation there is solely the fault of foolish state politicians and the people who continue to vote for them." That's actually more a criticism of California Democrats than of Bush. And then there was this: "Mr. Bush's long-term vision of developing fuel cells, ethanol, and other forms of power is right on. But, until those things become a reality, we must find all the natural gas and oil we can. That means drilling in sensitive areas while imposing strict environmental oversight." This is, in fact, support for Bush's policy of drilling

in the Arctic National Wildlife Refuge and other pristine areas. O'Reilly's closing advice: "President Bush must correct the terrible mistakes of Bill Clinton, and he's got to do it fast."

The same was true on his May 30, 2002, program, when O'Reilly teased this segment: "Next, the ACLU versus the Justice Department. Who is looking out for us? A debate in a moment." But there was no "debate" at all—just O'Reilly, a vociferous critic of ACLU, and former federal prosecutor Bill Otis, who agreed with him. He told O'Reilly that ACLU members are "basically misguided idealists in some ways. But I think you're right that it's the Department of Justice here that's looking out for us."

## Gays and Lesbians: Shut Up—You'll Thank Me for It

Though they agree on most issues, O'Reilly has taken heat from the far Right for not being as conservative as it would like. The gap between the two is perhaps widest when it comes to homosexuality, where the far Right finds O'Reilly far too accommodating. It's a dispute that O'Reilly enjoys airing in the open, as it might convince some viewers that his views are not uniformly in line with the Right.

> **"I believe that there is a lobby, and it's based around the gay lobby too, that wants to mainstream homosexuality and AIDS, because AIDS is obviously an offshoot of homosexual conduct in many instances." (7/15/02)**

But don't sign O'Reilly up for a PFLAG membership just yet. Much of the time, the distinction between the far Right's position on homosexuality and O'Reilly's own is almost none. During an interview with a lesbian activist, O'Reilly was adamant about keeping her at arm's length: "I wouldn't let you anywhere near my seven-year-old, with all due respect" (8/6/02). On one program, O'Reilly's Fox colleague Juan Williams criticized Boy Scouts of America for its antigay position, saying that a scout leader's "sexual conduct is not on display as he's leading these young men." O'Reilly's response: "How do you know? He might be wearing a tutu . . .

He can have the little Boy Scout uniform and tights. You don't know what he's doing" (7/2/00). O'Reilly is most worried about the effect gays and lesbians might have on children, despite the lack of evidence that gay people pose any threat to the young: "I want my kids to have a childhood. I don't want to have to explain to a seven-year-old why some guy dressed up like Dolly Parton is holding hands with a biker" (*Fort Lauderdale Sun-Sentinel*, 3/23/02). He was more succinct in his first book, writing: "Dykes on bikes? Take a hike!"

According to a profile in *Playboy* (5/1/02), a production meeting for O'Reilly's show offered this behind-the-scenes insight: "One producer wonders if a guest is fitting for television because she's 'an ugly lesbian.' O'Reilly winces at the idea of having the woman on the show, but not at the remark."

Even while defending against gays' being "deprived of basic rights," O'Reilly hardly comes across as a friend: "It is incumbent on homosexuals to accept the fact that their sexual proclivities are an aberration, a departure from the normal state of affairs," O'Reilly writes. "Some Americans believe this aberration is sinful, others think that it cannot be helped and is therefore acceptable in a secular society" (*Fort Lauderdale Sun-Sentinel*, 3/23/02).

But what really seems to set him off the most is the idea that he might actually see gay people being gay in public: "That's my advice to all homosexuals, whether they're in the Boy Scouts, or in the Army, or in high school: Shut up, don't tell anybody what you do, your life will be a lot easier" (7/7/00).

O'Reilly imagines ulterior motives lurking behind a homosexual's decision to come out, motives he argues make gays and lesbians no better than the bigots who hate them. As he explained in one commentary,

> ## O'REILLY ON GAY PRIDE PARADES:
>
> **"People who see that have a right to not like homosexuals the way they're being portrayed in the parade. . . . They have an absolute right to condemn that behavior, to say it's corrupting to my children, I don't want them to see it, and if this is what the gay pride thing is all about, then *blank* them."**
> **(7/2/02)**

"The no-spin on this, however, is the hidden agenda. 'Talking Points' believes that the root of most public displays by homosexuals is anger, anger that some Americans will not accept their lifestyle. Rejection is never easy, but it is a part of life . . . If gay people would learn that lesson, their lives would become easier" (8/30/02).

O'Reilly continues: "If gays think they will gain acceptance by flaunting their sexuality, they're crazy. All that does is make more people dislike them. It is self-destructive, unclassy, and illogical. So what these public sexual displays are really meant to do is offend people that don't like gays—that gays don't like, I should say. They are personal attacks on opponents of homosexuality. That's the no-spin truth of the matter."

O'Reilly thus concludes his lesson about how gays can be the real oppressors: "But what many gays don't realize is that some Americans who live and let live are angered because their children are being exposed to situations far beyond their years. And when gay activists say that's tough, that kids should be forced to deal with homosexuality at an early age, then those activists become the oppressors. Those people become just like the homophobes they despise." With those stirring words, O'Reilly gives hope to oppressed heterosexuals everywhere.

## The Racism Factor?

**We do more reporting on race on *The Factor* than any other program in America. (10/14/02)**

Given O'Reilly's obsession with Jesse Jackson, his criticism of reparations for slavery, his frustration with the absence of leaders in the black community whom he approves of, and his unflinching hostility towards hiphop culture ("whatever that is," he once mocked), the above statement is probably true. And it's precisely his mostly negative treatment of race issues that has caused some of O'Reilly's critics to wonder if he's racist.

The accusation infuriates him; as he vented in a March 1, 2003, column: "If you can't win the debate, smear your opponent. That's an old political trick that has been elevated by pressure groups to strategy No. 1. . . . All of us must realize that racial demonization is now organized and well funded, and it will not end until everyday people begin condemning it. . . . Using the race card to frighten the press hurts us all."

But are O'Reilly's critics using the so-called race card, or is there something about O'Reilly that lends credence to the charges of racism? Of course, O'Reilly might have an unusual opinion of what constitutes racism. After Representative Charles Rangel (Democrat, New York) warned that faith-based government funding might "go to a white Southern racist school" (7/2/02), O'Reilly countered, "There aren't any white Southern racist schools!" What about Bob Jones University? O'Reilly scoffed: "Come on! Oh, God . . . it's a fundamentalist school. I wouldn't call it racist." Others might disagree: The school only lifted its long-standing

## It's Not Racism

"Now, the greatest misconception, in my opinion, that black people have about whites is that some whites don't like them because of the color of their skin. I don't know anybody who thinks that way, because somebody's black or somebody's red or somebody's brown, I immediately don't like them . . . I'll tell you what they don't like. I'll tell you what whites—and I'm taking this from my grandmother. . . . My grandmother didn't like black people because she was afraid of them. . . . All my grandmother saw were young black males on television getting arrested, right, she—when she rode the bus . . . in New York, she saw some black people being rowdy or whatever. . . . She was afraid. And because she was afraid, she didn't like them. So it's not the color of the skin that my grandmother didn't like, it was, 'I'm afraid'. . . . It had nothing to do with skin color." (8/11/00)

ban on interracial dating in the year 2000, provided that students had written permission from their parents (Associated Press, 3/8/00).

Since O'Reilly's "racism meter" might be tuned a little differently, let's consider three examples straight from O'Reilly's mouth:

There are certain names that O'Reilly seems to feel merit suspicion. When a public school in Oakland, California, came under fire for holding a forum on Iraq dominated by antiwar speakers, O'Reilly fired away at one of them: "You've got some pretty crazy guys here, is all I'm saying. Mohamed Mohamed, who has relatives in Iraq, is he an expert on what's going on, Mohamed Mohamed?" What might exclude Mohamed? O'Reilly never explained. "Well, does he have a Ph.D. in political science? Or what's his background, Mohamed Mohamed?" When O'Reilly's guest claimed that "he came from one of the local universities," O'Reilly was unimpressed: "Oh, come on!" (1/15/03)

During an interview for *Stuff* magazine, O'Reilly opined that "the most unattractive women in the world are probably in the Muslim countries." O'Reilly later insisted "there was no malice intended. It was just in jest" (*New York Daily News*, 10/10/02).

Searching for a word to describe someone who assists immigrants crossing the border, O'Reilly came up with a racial slur: "wetback." The incident was written off as an unfortunate gaffe, but a reporter from the *Morning Call* newspaper in Allentown, Pennsylvania, had reported O'Reilly using the same racist term in a speech earlier in the year: "O'Reilly criticized the Immigration and Naturalization Service for not doing its job and not keeping out 'the wetbacks.'" O'Reilly denied making the comment (*Washington Post*, 2/17/02), but the reporter stands by his account.

## Where Are the Black Leaders?

While O'Reilly criticizes African-American leaders for their supposed grandstanding on issues such as police brutality, he decries their lack of activism on issues he's concerned with. When five-year-old African-

American girl Rilya Wilson was missing in Florida, O'Reilly wondered, "Where are the nation's black leaders in this case? Where are Jesse Jackson, Al Sharpton, [NAACP head] Kweisi Mfume? Black Entertainment Television?"

O'Reilly elaborates on the problem: "We have black leaders in this country who blame everything on Whitey, everything's the system's fault, and that gives a built-in excuse to fail and act irresponsible. 'Oh, I can't get a job. Whitey won't let me,' or 'I can't get educated. The teachers are bad, so I'm going to go out and get high and sell drugs. That's the only way we can make money here.' You know what I mean? And it's a vicious cycle" (6/8/99).

But O'Reilly doesn't just offer criticisms of the black community; he's got solutions at the ready. In fact, O'Reilly has a model for new black leadership: former Republican Congressman J. C. Watts. "And I said to Congressman Watts, 'You should be Jesse Jackson. You should go and try to be the leader of American blacks.' In my opinion, this is the man that you guys should be embracing," O'Reilly explained to one guest (1/19/01). "He's an honest man . . . I think that you guys, the minority community, need a leader. And I think Watts is the guy to do it."

When not nominating his own leaders for African Americans, O'Reilly's eager to dispense other advice: "I don't understand why in the year 2000, with all of the media that we have, that a certain segment of the African-American community does not understand that they must aggressively pursue their child's welfare. That is they have to stop drinking, they have to stop taking drugs and boozing, and—and whites do it, too! Whites do it, too!" (1/17/00)

Still other incidents on O'Reilly's record suggest he owes more apologies than advice.

In April 2003, O'Reilly hosted a fund-raiser for Best Friends, a charity benefiting inner-city schoolchildren in the Washington, D.C., area. As reported in the *Washington Post* (4/15/03), O'Reilly was trying to fill the time

before a singing group called the Best Men was set to perform. O'Reilly joked, "Does anyone know where the Best Men are? I hope they're not in the parking lot stealing our hubcaps." Ouch. According to the *Post* report, some of the conservatives in the audience were aghast at the comment.

During a segment about black athletes suing over the minimum academic standards for college admission, O'Reilly told a guest, "Look, you know as well as I do most of these kids come out and they can't speak English" (2/9/00).

 **Will African Americans break away from the pack-thinking and reject immorality—because that's the reason the family's breaking apart: alcohol, drugs, infidelity. You have to reject that, and it doesn't seem—and I'm broadly speaking here, but a lot of African Americans won't reject it. (2/25/99)**

**I've been to Africa three times, all right? You can't bring Western reasoning into the culture, the same way you can't bring it into fundamental Islam. (5/6/02)**

Criticizing Democratic politicians for meeting with Al Sharpton, O'Reilly compared him to racist former KKK member David Duke, saying, "Why would it be different? Both use race to promote themselves" (3/16/00). O'Reilly also equated the Black Panthers with David Duke: "You were promoting your people, black people, and he's promoting white people. So what's the difference?" (1/11/99)

Discussing affirmative action and reparations for slavery: "Get off the abuse excuse. Get off the pity party and black Americans will prosper" (1/16/03). To O'Reilly, the movement for reparations "is baloney. You don't need that money. What you need in the inner cities is discipline." Racial profiling by the police is "emotional, of course, but a bogus issue."

# The Reds Are Coming!

Like some other conservatives, O'Reilly frets over the threat posed by communism and socialism, and imagines those ideas are polluting the American political mainstream.

## America's tax code veers dangerously close to socialism:

Once the feds start to redistribute wealth, start to punish wealthy people by imposing draconian taxes, then we're out of the free-enterprise system and into quasi-socialism. (2/19/02)

Some Americans continue to believe that communism and socialism can be good things. We can see this every day as our government strives to redistribute income by levying punishing tax rates on the wealthy. (4/28/00)

## One politician offers hope:

President Bush rightly recognizes that creeping socialism blunts individual motivation and goes against the Founding Fathers' idea of unfettered competition. (2/8/01)

## During the 2000 Democratic primary, voters had a choice between two different varieties of socialism:

Al Gore: "Now for the top story tonight: Is Al Gore running for president on a quasi-socialistic platform—in this case, socialism being defined as work and production being supervised by the government?" (6/7/00)

Bill Bradley: "The senator's message is very close to socialism, but many Americans have no problem with that" (2/11/00).

**On his own program, O'Reilly played this clip of himself on THE TONIGHT SHOW with Jay Leno:**

I just feel that Hillary is a socialist, you know, and I'm paying enough tax. . . . Hillary wants to take my money, your money, and Freddie's money, and give it to strangers. She's going to take our money . . . she's coming to your house, going to take your wallet right out of there. (5/21/02)

After playing the clip, O'Reilly proudly elaborated on his rant:

Now, some people say I'm misguided. Mrs. Clinton is certainly not a socialist, that extreme. But they're wrong . . . she will run for president in the year 2008 on the Democratic ticket, which 'Talking Points' has now renamed the Democratic Socialist ticket."

A few weeks before O'Reilly's statements, Clinton was one of just a handful of Democrats backing stricter work requirements for welfare recipients (*New York Times*, 5/3/02).

## Elsewhere in the world:

"Now, [Germany's Prime Minister] Joschka Fisher, a guy who has a long history of being a radical and an anti-American and a communist sympathizer, is the second most powerful man in the country." (2/20/03)

What's happened in Canada in the recent years is that you've become increasingly socialistic and left-wing, and we haven't. . . . Look at your taxation rate. Look at your entitlements . . . Look at all of that . . . Look at [Prime Minister Jean] Chretien. Look at your leader! (1/29/03)

The problem with Canada is that their president is to the left of the American people: "The facts speak for themselves. You're looking at a man here who's a quasi-socialist. You elected him. He's the problem, because this country is going further to the right" (1/29/03).

# The O'Reilly Fact-Check

**Opinions are fine as long as they are backed up with facts, but a distortion of the facts will always be stopped dead by me.** (9/9/02)

**O**f course, there's nothing wrong with being a conservative commentator. The problem is when you're disingenuous about your politics and twist the facts to suit them. If it's spin to back up your arguments with bogus facts and statistics, and to dismiss numbers that don't fit in with your preconceptions, then *The O'Reilly Factor* isn't a "No-Spin Zone"—it's Spin City.

## All Things American

 **O'REILLY:** O'Reilly went to unusual lengths to argue that injecting some religion into public life would not violate the Constitution, which only prohibits promotion of one particular religion: "We went through it, you know, line by line, and the establishment clause clearly says 'the establishment of a religion,' singular." When O'Reilly's guest disagreed, "I think it says respecting an 'establishment of religion.' It doesn't say 'a religion,'" O'Reilly stood firm on his shaky ground: "Yes, it says 'a religion'"(2/25/02).

**OH REALLY?** His guest was correct. The Constitution's establishment clause states: "Congress shall make no law respecting an establishment of religion." Months later, O'Reilly's argument was unchanged: "The establishment clause clearly states that the United States will not promote a single religion and will not deny anybody freedom of religion—that's all" (1/31/03).

**? ? ?**

**O'REILLY:** Commenting on the Ninth Circuit Court of Appeals, which ruled that forcing students to say the Pledge of Allegiance was unconstitutional: "The reason they're even sitting there is because they were appointed by liberal politicians. Conservative politicians would never appoint the pinheads sitting on the Ninth Circuit" (3/4/03).

**OH REALLY?** The opinion in the Pledge of Allegiance case was drafted by Judge Alfred T. Goodwin, who was appointed by Richard Nixon.

**O'REILLY:** Explaining free speech rights to a high school student, who backed the establishment of a Satanic club at school: "They don't have any First Amendment rights. As soon as they walk in the door . . . Yes, they don't have any. Joe, do you realize that, as soon as you walk in the San Mateo High School door, you don't have any rights, that you have to do what the teachers tell you to do?" (10/2/02)

**OH REALLY?** "It can hardly be argued that either students or teachers shed their constitutional rights to freedom of speech . . . at the schoolhouse gates" (U.S. Supreme Court, *Tinker v. Des Moines*, 1969).

For the record, O'Reilly already knows this. When a high school student was suspended by his school for putting up pro-war flyers, he sued the school and won. O'Reilly had him on the show to cheer his legal victory: "A federal judge has ruled the school violated the boy's freedom of speech rights. The school administrators were ordered by the judge to undergo constitutional rights training, and the school board has been ordered to pay Aaron and his parents $3,000" (11/30/01). Maybe O'Reilly could get some of the same training.

### ? ? ?

 **O'REILLY:** "The Founders were not concerned with the minority rights, they were concerned with everybody's rights."

**OH REALLY?** "All, too, will bear in mind this sacred principle, that though the will of the majority is in all cases to prevail, that will, to be rightful, must be reasonable; that the minority possess their equal rights, which equal laws must protect, and to violate which would be oppression" (Thomas Jefferson, "First Inaugural Address," March 4, 1801).

### ? ? ?

 **O'REILLY:** Speaking to a guest about going to court: "You have to put your hand on the Bible. So hopefully, you'll never be arrested; but if you are, and you have to testify, you're going to have to put that hand on a Bible there, doctor, or you're going to be held in contempt of court" (3/15/02).

**OH REALLY?** According to the Federal Rules of Evidence, Rule 603, a witness is required to declare that he or she "will testify truthfully, by oath or affirmation administered in a form calculated to awaken the witness's conscience and impress the witness's mind with the duty to do so." A Bible isn't necessary; a note to the rule explains that the rule allows for "flexibility" in order to apply to atheists, conscientious objectors, and others.

### ? ? ?

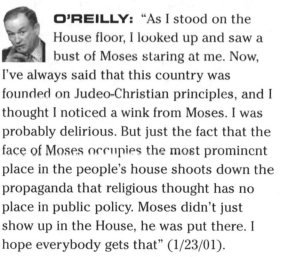 **O'REILLY:** "As I stood on the House floor, I looked up and saw a bust of Moses staring at me. Now, I've always said that this country was founded on Judeo-Christian principles, and I thought I noticed a wink from Moses. I was probably delirious. But just the fact that the face of Moses occupies the most prominent place in the people's house shoots down the propaganda that religious thought has no place in public policy. Moses didn't just show up in the House, he was put there. I hope everybody gets that" (1/23/01).

**OH REALLY?** Get this—Moses is just one of the twenty-three portraits in the House Chamber, which pay tribute to historical figures who influenced American law. Among the portraits is Hammurabi, the Babylonian king who lived hundreds of years before Moses. Also included in the "people's house," perhaps to O'Reilly's chagrin, is Napoleon.

## The Clinton Years

**O'REILLY:** "I never heard Mr. Clinton once say, come out and say, we need more discipline in the schools, we need tougher standards, we need alternative schools because we don't want the student body to be diverted by just a few. I never heard any of that" (3/27/01).

**OH REALLY?** "I have laid before the Congress a number of proposals that will make education our number-one priority and result in dramatic improvements of our schools: smaller classes, better teaching, higher standards, expanded choice, more discipline, greater accountability" (Bill Clinton, speech, 5/7/98).

**O'REILLY:** "I was stunned when Clinton won. Hillary knows nothing about New York and doesn't really care. She's been to Iowa eight times since she's been elected senator, and she has not been to Rochester, New York" (speech, Commonwealth Club, 10/17/01).

**OH REALLY?** Before O'Reilly's speech, Senator Clinton had made at least seven visits to the Rochester area since being elected (*Christian Science Monitor*, 8/22/01), including a visit in mid-August to open her Rochester office (*Rochester Democrat and Chronicle*, 8/16/01).

**? ? ?**

**O'REILLY:** "On Tuesday, we presented a story that said Senator Hillary Clinton has not attended any of the funerals of everyday victims of 9/11. The critical mail poured in. 'You don't like Hillary,' they wailed, 'leave her alone.' Nobody challenged the accuracy of the story" (11/29/01).

**OH REALLY?** Clinton attended the funeral of Sonia Morales Puopolo, who died at the World Trade Center (Associated Press, 10/6/01), and a memorial service at the Cathedral of St. John the Divine for seventy-nine workers missing from the Windows on the World restaurant (*New York Daily News*, 10/2/01).

## ? ? ?

**O'REILLY:** At the top of his February 11, 1999, show, at the height of the Clinton impeachment drama, O'Reilly explained that he was leaning towards acquittal until "a strange thing happened late yesterday. White House spokesman Joe Lockhart told the press that Mr. Clinton was no longer ready to embrace censure, a turnaround from December when Mr. Clinton said he was willing to accept censure." This turned O'Reilly around on the entire matter: "His flip-flop on censure has clearly sent me a message, and that is that President Clinton does not respect or even understand the laws of this country. Therefore, he is not able to faithfully execute them and has violated his presidential oath to do so. So my vote is for removal."

**OH REALLY?** O'Reilly received a message that no one was sending. Check the transcript from that day's press briefing:

> **LOCKHART: I think, as we've said for many months now, and the president has said, he would be open to some censure. He understands the wrongful nature of his behavior. But it is up to the Senate to make decisions on censure; whether they want to do it, how they want to do it, what the censure would be. And we'll leave it to the Senate to make those decisions.**

Lockhart went on to answer a number of other questions about censure the same way. Even O'Reilly's Fox News colleague, Brian Wilson, reported: "Presidential spokesman Joe Lockhart, treading softly, saying the president would still accept censure" (2/10/99).

**O'REILLY:** "Did you know the Feds handed out more than $32 million in performance bonuses to government workers during the last year of the Clinton administration? No wonder the deficit is back" (2/1/02).

**OH REALLY?** It's illogical to argue that the federal deficit in 2002 has anything to do with bonuses from the year 2000. For the record, the deficit at the time of O'Reilly's statement was estimated to be $106 billion (*New York Times*, 1/30/02).

## ? ? ?

**O'REILLY:** During the White House transition, O'Reilly helped hype some minor property damage by outgoing Clinton administration officials into an object lesson about Bill Clinton's morality: "I mean, the price tag right now is about $200,000 so that's a felony right there" (1/26/01).

**OH REALLY?** After many months of investigation, the final General Accounting Office report documented about $20,000 in damage (*Time*, 6/24/02), including some that could be attributed to general wear and tear.

**O'REILLY:** "Mr. Gore, you may remember, accepted illegal donations at a Buddhist temple in California. If we had had an honest attorney general instead of Janet Reno, Mr. Gore might be on parole right now. That is not an exaggeration" (5/15/02).

**OH REALLY?** The Justice Department official who recommended that an independent counsel investigate the incident at the Buddhist temple, Charles La Bella, would likely call it an exaggeration: "Most experienced prosecutors had the belief that many of these allegations, some very technical violations, even if they were committed, were not the types of violations that would result in a prosecution. They just weren't. Experienced prosecutors came to that conclusion" (*ABC News*, 6/11/00).

## ? ? ?

**O'REILLY:** When Kathleen Willey came forward and accused Bill Clinton of having made an unwanted sexual advance towards her in 1993, O'Reilly suggested that the incident had led to her husband's suicide: "I believe Kathleen Willey when she says that private detectives hounded her, that they tried to break her, that they tried to threaten her, and her husband committed suicide. This is another example of all of it emanating from Bill Clinton" (1/15/01).

**OH REALLY?** Willey's husband killed himself the day that the alleged incident took place. According to Willey, an investigation suggesting that her husband had embezzled from clients at his law firm were what contributed to his suicide—not pressure from Clinton's "private detectives."

## Watching the Competition

**O'REILLY:** "Ashcroft will never show up on Larry King and be asked about the Marc Rich pardon. Never in a million years" (*Playboy*, 5/1/02).

**OH REALLY?** My how time flies! Ashcroft was asked about the pardon in his very first interview with Larry King after he became attorney general: "Your thoughts on the Marc Rich pardon?" (CNN's *Larry King Live*, 2/7/01)

**O'REILLY:** On June 5, 2002, O'Reilly claimed that fifteen of the nineteen September 11 hijackers came to the United States through Canada. Though his guest questioned the assertion, O'Reilly stood firm: "Well, that was the report on *60 Minutes*, the transit right through. I don't know whether they lived there, but that was the report. Now, if it's wrong, it's wrong" (6/5/02).

**OH REALLY?** It's not *60 Minutes* that is wrong—it's O'Reilly. As CBS correspondent Steve Kroft reported, Canadian Deputy Prime Minister John Manley "is quick to point out that all of the September 11th hijackers were living in the United States with no connection to Canada" (*60 Minutes*, 4/28/02). O'Reilly's was apparently garbling this statement from Kroft: "Law enforcement authorities in Canada and abroad believe at least fifteen Islamic terrorists with connections to al Qaeda have operated here."

## Bungling the Numbers

ABC's John Stossel appeared on *The O'Reilly Factor* (1/26/01) and claimed that $40,000 in government money is spent annually on antipoverty programs for each poor family, echoing a claim from the Heritage Foundation's Robert Rector, who arrives at that figure by deceptively including expensive programs that also go to nonpoor families—such as Medicare, Pell grants, and reduced-price school lunches. A few days later, O'Reilly was exaggerating the already misleading figure: "We're paying $40,000 per person who [is] on government assistance now" (1/29/01). O'Reilly's change of "per family" to "per person" quadruples the amount of spending Stossel was claiming.

## ? ? ?

 **O'REILLY:** On one show (2/26/01), O'Reilly explained to Florida State Senator Kendrick Meek that, thanks to Governor Jeb Bush's "One Florida" program, 37 percent of students at Florida universities were black: "Thirty-seven percent. That's much higher than the population, the black population, of Florida. Bush is doing a good job for you guys and you're vilifying him." When Meek challenged those numbers, O'Reilly insisted they were "dead on."

**OH REALLY?** Dead wrong: Total *minority* enrollment for the freshman class entering in 2000 was 37 percent (*Jacksonville Florida Times-Union*, 8/30/00). Black enrollment was about 18 percent.

## France-Bashers Unite!

**O'REILLY:** To support his call for a boycott of French products for France's opposing the Iraq war, O'Reilly claimed that even "a big newspaper like the *Chicago Tribune* [is] saying that we should scorn the French" (3/17/03).

**OH REALLY?** The *Tribune*'s March 10, 2003, editorial, cheekily headlined "Bash the French? *Mais oui!*," did not actually support anything like O'Reilly's boycott and concluded that "the American public should think twice before swearing off all things French."

**O'REILLY:** "So Montana, $5 billion worth of French stock they're selling. Is that going to hurt France?" (3/25/03)

**OH REALLY?** As guest Bruce Upbin of *Forbes* magazine explained, the total amount that the state of Montana was selling was far lower: about $14 million. O'Reilly's "$5 billion" is the total size of the state's pension fund (Associated Press, 3/22/03). O'Reilly wasn't terribly convinced that he was wrong, though: "That's the number we had. That was—I guess they're selling—or moving around $5 billion because some of it's subsidies and things like that." Huh?

## ? ? ?

 **O'REILLY:** O'Reilly dug up recent history to find more reasons to dislike the French: "You remember that France opposed bombing Serbia, even though soldiers from that country were committing mass murder throughout the Balkans. Mr. Clinton, to his credit, ignored French objections and bombed Belgrade" (3/14/03). Days later, O'Reilly repeated:

"You'll remember President Clinton avoided the UN, ignored the objections of France, and under the banner of NATO destroyed the infrastructure of Milosevic's government, leading to a regime change" (3/18/03).

**OH REALLY?** The French not only supported the bombing of Serbia, but also participated in it, providing the second-largest air force in the NATO air campaign, behind the United States.

## Stop Eminem!

**O'REILLY:** Complaining to www.stopdrlaura.com's John Aravosis, a critic of TV personality Dr. Laura Schlessinger: "There is no eminem.com, stopeminem.com. There is no picketing of the label" (2/21/01).

**OH REALLY?** The very night O'Reilly made his claim, activists protested outside the Grammy awards to draw attention to Eminem's misogyny and homophobia. The protests, some led by the Gay & Lesbian Alliance Against Defamation (GLAAD), had been active for months. But O'Reilly should have already known this: about a month earlier (1/4/01), *Spin* magazine's Alan Light had clued him in:

> O'REILLY: It's clear he's calling homosexuals bad names and saying that they're deviant people, which he is. Why isn't the homosexuality lobby picketing Eminem?
>
> LIGHT: Well, the homosexual lobby is picketing Eminem.
>
> O'REILLY: Where? I didn't see it. The Grammys are coming up again.
>
> LIGHT: Oh, he's being protested. There's all kinds of protests. Gay and lesbian activists in GLAAD . . .
>
> O'REILLY: Didn't see it. Haven't seen it.
>
> LIGHT: They are. They protested the MTV awards. They'll be protesting at the Grammys.
>
> O'REILLY: All right, I'll believe you.

## Politically Correct Pick

**O'REILLY:** When slain gay rights activist and San Francisco City Supervisor Harvey Milk was named to *Time* magazine's "100 Persons of the Century" list, O'Reilly was miffed. "Looks like a politically correct pick to me," O'Reilly opined, saying that Milk "was in the forefront of that 'Hey, let's have sex with eighty guys.'" O'Reilly added that Milk "was killed by another homosexual, though" (6/7/99).

**OH REALLY?** Milk was killed by former Supervisor Dan White, a heterosexual who opposed gay activism: "White steadfastly opposed every street closing or permit that involved gays," Randy Shilts noted in his biography of Milk, *The Mayor of Castro Street* (St. Martin's, 1982).

## No Culture

 **O'REILLY:** When Madeline Toogood was caught on a security camera hitting her child in the backseat of her car, some in the media focused on Toogood's ethnic heritage as an Irish Traveler. Here's O'Reilly's take: "Whoa, whoa, I don't believe that Irish Travelers is a culture. I believe it's a group, a cult that band together for whatever purpose. I'm Irish, and I travel, all right? But I'm not an Irish Traveler. . . . You're saying that this is some kind of ethnic group. It's not" (9/26/02).

**OH REALLY?** O'Reilly admits that his opinion isn't rooted in any actual knowledge of the subject: "I didn't even know who these Irish Travelers were up until a week ago." The Irish Travelers are in fact an "ethnically distinct" nomadic group who speak their own language, often called Shelta (*Chicago Tribune*, 3/3/02).

## Health Care Baloney

**O'REILLY:** In response to guest Paul Loeb's claim that "We've got fifty million people without health care": "Oh, that's a lot of baloney . . . If you walk into any emergency room in this country, you get treated for free. Everybody gets it, all right. This myth that we have people starving, bleeding in the streets, is a bunch of garbage" (5/2/01).

**OH REALLY?** Analyzing data from the 1987 National Medical Expenditure Survey—at a time when fewer Americans lacked health insurance than today—David Himmelstein and Steffie Woolhandler concluded that 945,000 people were unable to receive emergency care that year (*American Journal of Public Health*, 3/95). Almost two-thirds of those unable to obtain care cited "high costs or lack of insurance."

## Middle East

 **O'REILLY:** O'Reilly rewrote diplomatic history during an interview with James Zogby of the Arab American Institute. After Zogby argued that Israeli settlements were an obstacle to peace between Israel and Palestine, O'Reilly countered that during the Camp David negotiations in July 2000, the offer made by Israeli Prime Minister Ehud Barak "would have given 90 percent of those settlements back"—an idea he credited to "what every single American expert who has seen that says" (4/2/02).

**OH REALLY?** In fact, O'Reilly got the proportion of settlements Barak was prepared to give up almost backwards: Barak promised Israelis that any deal with the Palestinians would involve keeping "80 percent of the settlers in settlement blocks under our sovereignty" (*Jerusalem Post*, 9/13/00). When Zogby pointed out O'Reilly's error, the host said he would welcome any former diplomats who could prove him wrong: "I'll put them on tomorrow," he said—but he didn't.

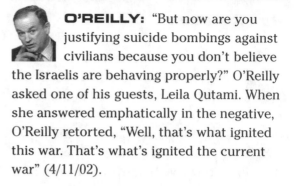 **O'REILLY:** "But now are you justifying suicide bombings against civilians because you don't believe the Israelis are behaving properly?" O'Reilly asked one of his guests, Leila Qutami. When she answered emphatically in the negative, O'Reilly retorted, "Well, that's what ignited this war. That's what's ignited the current war" (4/11/02).

**OH REALLY?** As Qutami tried to explain, the second intifada was "ignited" not by suicide bombings, but in the aftermath of a September 28, 2000, visit to Jerusalem's Temple Mount by Ariel Sharon (who would later become prime minister of Israel). Palestinians protested the visit to the holy site as having been a provocation—Sharon was accompanied by a large security contingent—and several Palestinians were killed in the ensuing days of violence. A tally of suicide attacks in Israel on the Israeli Foreign Ministry's website does not list any attacks between October 1998 and November 2000. The first suicide attack in the occupied territories (West Bank and Gaza Strip) came a month after Sharon's visit.

# Attacking the Academy

**O'REILLY:** "More than 80 percent of those teaching at Ivy League colleges in the USA voted for Al Gore," O'Reilly told an audience at Harvard. "Eighty-two percent of all Ivy League professors voted for Al Gore. OK?" (5/6/02)

**OH REALLY?** The poll O'Reilly is referring to was the work of Republican pollster and strategist Frank Luntz, conducted on behalf of conservative activist David Horowitz. It wasn't a poll of "all Ivy League professors," as O'Reilly claimed. Luntz polled 151 professors exclusively from the social sciences and the humanities faculties—where one might expect to find academics of a more liberal persuasion.

## ? ? ?

**O'REILLY:** Judith Levine's controversial 2002 book *Harmful to Minors: The Perils of Protecting Children from Sex* (University of Minnesota Press) was a popular topic on *The O'Reilly Factor*; O'Reilly's criticism focused largely on one apparently disturbing passage from Levine's book: "We relish our erotic attraction to children." As O'Reilly put it, "that is a dominant theme of the book . . . that we adults in America relish sexual contact with children. It's abhorrent" (4/18/02).

**OH REALLY?** That's in Levine's book—but she didn't write it. The guest on that segment was *Minneapolis Star Tribune* reporter Kristin Tillotson. After the show, she went back to check on O'Reilly's claim. Not surprisingly, he was mistaken. As Tillotson wrote of that passage:

> **Two problems: a) Levine didn't write those words; she was citing another author, and b) if you read the entire paragraph, you get a much different meaning: "'We relish our erotic attraction to children,' says Kincaid (witness the child beauty pageants in which JonBenet Ramsey was entered). But we also find that attraction abhorrent (witness the public shock and disgust at JonBenet's 'sexualization' in those pageants)." (*Minneapolis Star Tribune, 4/28/02*)**

## Lights Out in California

**O'REILLY:** "Many California politicians were afraid to anger environmentalist groups, so they didn't build any new power plants out here for twelve years" (3/27/01).

**OH REALLY?** Both parts of O'Reilly's claim are wrong. First, power plants were built in the 1990s in California. As Ralph Nader's nonprofit group Public Citizen reports, "In the 1990s before the state's electricity generation industry was restructured, the California Energy Commission certified twelve new power plants. Of these, three were never built. Nine plants are now in operation producing 952 megawatts of generation." And the *Los Angeles Daily News* reported that the energy companies were behind the decision not to build some of the twelve proposed plants: "Six years ago, Southern California Edison and other utilities helped kill a state plan that would have authorized the creation of new power plants sufficient to power 1.4 million homes" (1/21/01).

## Drilling in Alaska

**O'REILLY:** On *Fox News Sunday*, O'Reilly was on hand to question Democratic National Committee chairman Terry McAuliffe, who claimed that drilling in the Arctic National Wildlife Refuge "will give us nine months of supply. Is it worth going up there and risking the Arctic wilderness for nine months of supply?" (8/5/01) O'Reilly snapped back: "Hold it. That's been debunked by *Newsweek* magazine this week."

**OH REALLY?** That issue of *Newsweek* (8/13/01) didn't "debunk" anything: "Nobody really knows how much petroleum there is under the ANWR coastal plain," the magazine reported, citing a study by the U.S. Geological Survey that gave a wide range of possibilities. At the low end is "3.2 billion barrels of oil—less than half of what the United States burns in a single year." Newsweek reported that other estimates were higher, but that high oil prices would be necessary in order to make the drilling worth the economic risk for oil companies. Ever the environmentalist, O'Reilly reformulated the question this way: "Well, wait a minute. We're putting caribou and birds over the welfare of the American people—is [that] what you're doing? Right?"

## Fighting Terrorism

After the September 11 attacks:

 **O'REILLY:** "The telling event here is that faced with a violent faction using the name of Allah to kill civilians, Muslims the world over did little. There were no mass demonstrations against terrorism, no peace vigils, and no organized condemnation of the al Qaeda criminals" (8/1/02).

**OH REALLY?** There was a candlelight vigil in Iran shortly after the attacks, attended by "more than three thousand mostly young people" (*New York Times*, 9/21/01). A few days earlier, the *Times* reported that "thousands of people attending a World Cup qualifying match between Bahrain and Iran observed a moment of silence" (9/15/01). Palestinians gathered for a candlelight vigil in Jerusalem (*Baltimore Sun*, 9/15/01), and as NPR reported, "Most Arab leaders were quick to denounce the attacks. Jordan's King Hussein, Egyptian President Hosni Mubarak, and Lebanese Prime Minister Rafik Hariri sent their condolences. Officials in Syria, Kuwait, and other Gulf nations expressed sympathy for the American people and the families of the victims. Libyan leader Moammar Gadhafi said his country was ready to send aid to the United States" (9/12/01).

### ? ? ?

 **O'REILLY:** Explaining to one guest that accused traitors should not be tried in open civilian courts: "You are using the Constitution as a rubber band to stretch around an area that the Constitution just doesn't deal with. And that is Americans turning against their country, going to another country, and fighting against us. . . . [The] Constitution doesn't address it" (1/9/03).

**OH REALLY?** Article 3, Section III, of the Constitution says: "Treason against the United States, shall consist only in levying War against them, or in adhering to their Enemies, giving them Aid and Comfort. No Person shall be convicted of Treason unless on the Testimony of two Witnesses to the same overt Act, or on Confession in open Court."

## ? ? ?

 **O'REILLY:** New Jersey Poet Laureate Amiri Baraka became the object of controversy in September 2002 when it was revealed that his poem "Someone Blew Up America" included a reference to the fraudulent claim that Jewish employees at the World Trade Center had been warned not to go to work on September 11. O'Reilly tried to pin some of the blame for Baraka's words on New Jersey's Democratic Governor Jim McGreevey. O'Reilly claimed that Baraka was "appointed by a governor, a Democratic governor, to be the poet laureate," adding: "Governor McGreevey is the guy who appointed this pinhead" (9/30/02).

**OH REALLY?** As was widely reported, Baraka was not appointed by McGreevey but was "selected by a committee convened by the New Jersey Council for the Humanities and the State Council on the Arts" (*New York Times*, 9/28/02). At the time of O'Reilly's segment, McGreevey was trying to force Baraka out of the position but had no power to do so.

## ? ? ?

**O'REILLY:** In September 2002, when Eunice Stone reported to authorities that she may have overheard some young Arab men discussing a terror plot in a Georgia restaurant, O'Reilly made Stone out to be a hero—even after the men turned out to have no connection to terrorism. "Everybody admits there was talk about terrorism," O'Reilly explained. "The men say it was just a joke, but, obviously, Ms. Stone saw it differently" (9/16/02).

**OH REALLY?** After their release, the men denied talking about terrorism, even as a "joke." One of the students, Kambiz Butt, explained at a news conference on September 15, 2002, "Not once did we mention 9/11. . . . Nor did we joke about anything of that sort." His account was printed in the *New York Times* the same day that O'Reilly was still insisting the men had admitted to playing a joke.

## Crime in New York

 **O'REILLY:** In February 1999, African immigrant Amadou Diallo was killed by members of the Street Crime Unit, a plainclothes New York Police Department patrol. O'Reilly framed the issue as a trade-off for minority communities: either accept a heavy police presence in the neighborhood, or suffer the consequences. "We have a situation in New York here—and I'm sure you're aware of this—where the police got in a lot of trouble after the Diallo shooting, and they broke down the whole unit. . . . Well, what happened? The homicide rate in those neighborhoods went up 30, 50 percent in a matter of weeks" (10/12/99).

**OH REALLY?** In the first six months of 1999, the murder rate in New York increased 11.6 percent from the prior year. But in the Bronx, where Diallo was gunned down, the murder rate decreased 19.7 percent (*New York Post*, 7/7/99). There was a small increase in the citywide murder rate by the time O'Reilly gave his statistics (*New York Daily News*, 9/30/99), but in the Bronx, the murder rate had actually fallen 17.6 percent.

## We Didn't, Did We?

**O'REILLY:** Discussing a 1994 nuclear agreement between the United States and North Korea: "We didn't break any promises to the North Koreans as far as I know from the treaty that Bill Clinton signed in 1994. We kept our end of the bargain, yet they threw the UN inspectors out unilaterally with no provocation at all" (1/6/03).

**OH REALLY?** If O'Reilly had read the *Los Angeles Times* that morning, he may have been better prepared: "Under a 1994 agreement, the United States was supposed to build the North Koreans two safe light-water nuclear reactors and supply fuel oil in return for North Korea's freezing its nuclear program." The paper reported that "the reactors are years behind schedule," adding that

North Koreans "note—correctly—that the two light-water reactors under construction by an international consortium were supposed to be finished this year but are so far behind schedule that, at the current pace, they would not be completed until 2008."

## Attacking the ACLU

 **O'REILLY:** "Earlier this week, we reported on a kid who wore a T-shirt into a high school that had a picture of George Bush and 'International Terrorist' on it. The school sent him home, said you can't wear that here, and the ACLU, of course, is supporting the kid's right to do it, all right. . . . talk about hypocrisy. If the kid came in with an aborted fetus on his shirt, ACLU wouldn't be involved" (2/25/03).

**OH REALLY?** Why not? The ACLU of Ohio supported a preacher's lawsuit against the city of Cuyahoga Falls after he was charged with disorderly conduct after walking in a parade "with a placard that displayed an enlarged full-color photo of an aborted fetus" (Associated Press, 6/25/02).

 **O'REILLY:** "Using tactics the Taliban would admire, the ACLU has imposed the following on the American people," O'Reilly complained as he described several instances where the ACLU objected to public displays of religion. "In Breaux Bridge, Louisiana, the ACLU wants St. Martin Parish to take down all nativity scenes assembled in any church. In Billings, Montana, the ACLU has petitioned officials in Custer County to ban the nativity scene alto-gether. So you get the picture. It may be Christmas time, but don't display images of Christ or his parents in public or the ACLU may sue. This, of course, is fascism, not freedom" (12/2/02).

**OH REALLY?** First of all, maintaining a secular state is certainly not a tactic the Taliban—who set up an Islamic state—would "admire." O'Reilly is wrong on the facts when it comes to his examples of the ACLU's misdeeds. In Billings, Montana, the ACLU did not seek to "ban the nativity scene alto-gether." It sought to remove the scene from government property. In Breaux Bridge, Louisiana, the issue was not "all nativity scenes assembled in any church" but nativity scenes placed in a public park and on courthouse grounds (Associated Press, 12/19/01, 12/25/01). The ACLU of Louisiana never took legal action on the matter.

## Backing Bush

 **O'REILLY:** "And the winner is George W. Bush in Florida, at least according to the Knight Ridder newspaper chain . . . spearheaded by the *Miami Herald* and *USA Today*, the recount looked at the undervote, ballots that were rejected by Florida voting machines because punch holes were not clear. Mr. Bush emerged as the clear winner when those undervotes were counted" (4/4/01).

**OH REALLY?** The "clear winner"? The recount provided outcomes for the Florida ballots based on four different standards. Under three scenarios, Bush would have prevailed; under a more lenient standard, Gore came out ahead by three votes. But *USA Today* also found that the official hand-counts in seven Florida counties, completed before the U.S. Supreme Court stepped in, had missed hundreds, and perhaps even thousands, of potential Gore votes. If those votes had been properly counted, Gore would have won the entire state by three to four hundred votes under two of the four counting standards used to determine valid votes. (Those findings were reported exclusively on the paper's website.)

### ? ? ?

**O'REILLY:** Speaking about George W. Bush's controversial sale of Harken stock in 1990: "Bush was cleared by an SEC investigation of any wrongdoing" (7/8/02).

**OH REALLY:** The U.S. Securities and Exchange Commission investigations ended with a 1991 letter that stated that it "must in no way be construed as indicating that [George W. Bush] has been exonerated."

# O'Reilly on Drugs

**O'REILLY:** "With all due respect, professor, you know and I know that drug addicts are not thrown into prison. It is the dope dealer who goes" (6/3/02).

**OH REALLY?** That's an odd claim. In California alone, the state's Department of Corrections reported in April 2002 that eight thousand people had been admitted to prison for simple drug possession in 2001.

# ? ? ?

**O'REILLY:** When guest Joanne Page said that "so many of the people doing time under Rockefeller drug laws are there for simple possession," O'Reilly barked, "That's not true . . . you are basically calling every district attorney in New York a liar" (5/10/02).

**OH REALLY?** According to a review of 1997 New York state incarceration data by Human Rights Watch, "One in four drug offenders in prison was convicted of simple possession, primarily of minute quantities" (1/7/99).

# Taxing the Truth

**O'REILLY:** "According to the Census Bureau, the average American pays twice as much federal tax now as it did in 1985 under President Reagan" (1/19/99).

**OH REALLY?** The Census Bureau's figures on mean taxes paid do show the tax burden roughly doubling in that time period—from $4,675 in 1985 to $9,445 in 1997. But that's only if you don't consider inflation. If you make that crucial adjustment (shown in a different column in the same Census Bureau table), O'Reilly's increase largely vanishes: in 2001 dollars, the average income tax paid was $7,335 in 1985 and $10,388 in 1997. But that's not the only problem with O'Reilly's claim. Since income levels were also rising, a somewhat more accurate measure of tax burden would be the percentage of a person's income that goes to federal taxes. By that measure, the same census table shows that the income tax rate has risen only slightly as a percentage of income—about 2 percent in the period during which O'Reilly claims that taxes have doubled.

# Terror and Ecstasy

On February 4, 2002, Ethan Nadelmann of the Drug Policy Alliance questioned whether casual drug users were really funding terrorism, as O'Reilly was arguing. When Nadelmann pointed out that marijuana and Ecstasy were not involved in Afghanistan, O'Reilly responded, "Well, Ecstasy is," adding that "most comes from Holland."

To Nadelmann's retort—"And are the Dutch involved in terrorism?"—O'Reilly said, "No, but it's not run by the Dutch, it's run by Middle Eastern guys." When Nadelmann expressed incredulity, O'Reilly challenged him to a $100 wager, which the drug reform advocate accepted.

Later in the show, Nadelmann again asserted that the casual use of drugs such as marijuana and Ecstasy has "no link to the terrorists." "You're wrong about the Ecstasy," O'Reilly insisted. "You'll send me the check, and I'll be very happy. . . . It's controlled by Middle Eastern people out of Holland, that's where it comes in here from."

The following night, O'Reilly gloated that he had won the bet: "OK, here's what the Office of the National Drug Control Policy says, and we quote: 'Drug Enforcement Agency reporting demonstrates the involvement of Israeli criminal organizations in Ecstasy smuggling. Some of these individuals are of Russian and Georgian descent and have Middle Eastern ties'" (2/5/02).

O'Reilly seized on this mention of "Middle Eastern ties" to claim that federal drug officials backed up his claims. But the statement made no mention of Afghanistan or terrorism, the aspects of O'Reilly's claim that Nadelmann had most taken issue with. Is O'Reilly really claiming that Ecstasy users are supporting terrorism by giving money to Israeli mobsters? More likely he's just demonstrating once again that he'll clutch at any straw to avoid admitting that he's wrong.

73

It should also be pointed out that using "average" tax rates can yield deceptive results; since the rich pay more in income taxes, their tax bill will skew the "average" tax rate upward (see the Center on Budget and Policy Priorities' report *Information and Misinformation about Federal Tax Burdens*, at www.cbpp.org). Data from the Congressional Budget Office show that the *median* tax rate has been relatively stable over the past few decades. As the *Christian Science Monitor* reported, "the federal tax burden of a typical family is almost unchanged from 1977" (3/30/98). The CBPP's analysis of Congressional Budget Office data showed that households in the middle fifth of the income spectrum paid $7,100 in all federal taxes in 1985 and $7,890 in 1997.

## ? ? ?

After George W. Bush became president, the centerpiece of his domestic agenda was a massive tax cut tilted towards the wealthy. It was an issue close to O'Reilly's heart, and he vigorously defended Bush against critics of the cut.

 **O'REILLY:** Nancy Duff Campbell of the National Women's Law Center told O'Reilly, "One percent of the population is going to get about 40 percent of the tax cuts here. And they actually only pay about 20 percent." O'Reilly interrupted: "No, no, no that's not true . . . Ms. Campbell, I'm not going to let you get away with this. No-Spin Zone. We are taking [numbers from] the Tax Foundation, which is not a liberal group, where you guys take it from a liberal group. This is a nonpartisan think tank . . . it's not 20 percent. It is 33 percent."

**OH REALLY?** In this case, it was O'Reilly's guest who was trying to keep things spin-free. The deceptive 33 percent figure includes only income taxes, and not those such as the estate tax that fall disproportionately on the wealthy (Center on Budget and Policy Priorities, 2/7/01).

**O'REILLY:** After Bush's State of the Union address: "Bush's stats last night—I'm going to read them to the audience so there's no misunderstanding. Bush's stats last night were correct. I mean, he brought it down to, like, $1,600 goes to most working-class American families" (2/28/01).

**OH REALLY?** Just because Bush said it doesn't make it true. Citizens for Tax Justice pointed out that "almost 90 percent of taxpayers would receive less than $1,600 in tax cuts" and calculated that the "typical married couple filing jointly would receive an income tax cut of $1,028 under the Bush plan, when it is fully in place in 2006." As *USA Today*'s Walter Shapiro pointed out, Bush's claim was "as deceptive as a 'you've already won' sweepstakes mailing" (2/7/01).

### ? ? ?

**O'REILLY:** "Thirty-seven percent of Americans pay no federal income tax at all because of the Earned Income Tax Credit" (1/6/03).

**OH REALLY?** It's true that about one-third of Americans pay no federal income tax, but the Earned Income Tax Credit is not the reason why. The 37 percent figure includes nonfilers, who obviously do not get tax credits. And according to analysis by the Center on Budget and Policy Priorities, fewer than half of tax filers who owe no income taxes received the tax credit in 2001. So of Americans who owe no income tax, only about one third receive the Earned Income Tax Credit.

### ? ? ?

**O'REILLY:** In response to Reverend Al Sharpton's criticisms of the Bush tax cut: "Oh, that's propaganda. You know nobody buys that. Are you going to still do that? Tax cuts to the wealthy? Are you going to still bang that mantra? Nobody buys that stuff" (11/7/02).

**OH REALLY?** According to a CBS–*New York Times* poll, plenty of people were buying it: 56 percent of respondents believed Bush's tax cuts benefit the wealthy. As CBS reported on the *Early Show*, "a majority of Americans say the Bush tax cuts are unfair because they favor the rich" (3/14/01).

# ? ? ?

After Bush got his first round of tax cuts, he proposed more. This time the centerpiece was the elimination of the tax on stock dividends. As he had done the first time around, O'Reilly made sure that the naysayers were stopped dead in their tracks.

 **O'REILLY:** When Larry Mishel of the Economic Policy Institute remarked, "I see that most of the benefits and most of the people who benefit from this are only going to be those people in the upper 20 percent, perhaps even the upper 5 percent," O'Reilly resorted to a low-grade insult: "Listen, Mr. Mishel, you're either lying or can't read, one of the two."

**OH REALLY?** The idea that Bush's tax cut plan is skewed towards the rich isn't even debatable. According to the Tax Policy Center, about half of tax filers would receive $100 or less. Citizens for Tax Justice found that "three-fifths of Bush's proposed tax reductions for this year would go to the best-off 10 percent of all taxpayers" (1/7/03).

 **O'REILLY:** "According to the Tax Foundation, the average American working person works three hours out of eight each day in order to pay his or her federal taxes" (*The No Spin Zone*, p. 112).

**OH REALLY?** The "three hours" calculation is for all taxes—federal, state, and local—not just federal.

# ? ? ?

**O'REILLY:** "Today, July 6, is the first day the average American is working for himself. Up until today, everything you've earned will go to the government. From now on, you get to keep your salary. This, of course, is insane" (7/6/01).

**OH REALLY?** Another misleading citation. July 6 was designated by the conservative group Americans for Tax Reform as "Cost of Government Day." But the cost calculation is not just based on money that will "go to the government." It is based on taxes plus "the cost of regulation," such as requirements for safety labels, which the group argues make life more expensive.

**O'REILLY:** Talking about city income tax: "Nobody has one except the Big Apple."

**OH REALLY?** Plenty of other cities have a personal income tax. Detroit, for example, has had one for decades (*Detroit News*, 7/7/02), and Cincinnati has had one since 1988.

## The Words of the Founding Fathers?

**O'REILLY:** O'Reilly sought to bolster his case that the Founding Fathers were inspired by their Christian faith by digging up some valuable quotes. This one from Thomas Jefferson seemed to clinch the matter for O'Reilly: "This is a prayer, a public prayer. National prayer for peace that Jefferson wrote himself: 'Almighty God, Who has given us this good land for our heritage; We humbly beseech Thee that we may always prove ourselves a people mindful of Thy favor and glad to do Thy will. Bless our land with honorable ministry, sound learning, and pure manners'" (2/19/03).

**OH REALLY?** This Jefferson quote is often cited—and inaccurate. According to the Jefferson Library, there's never been any documentation that it was ever written or spoken by Thomas Jefferson.

## Polling Abuse: Factoring Fertik

On September 24, 2002, O'Reilly's interview with Bob Fertik of www. democrats.com was a comedy of errors. Here's how the trouble started:

**FERTIK: The majority of Americans oppose this war in Iraq.**

**O'REILLY: No, they don't. . . . Now, Mr. Fertik you're either being untruthful or naive. Yesterday a CNN-Gallup poll comes out, 66 percent of Americans support going into Iraq, even without UN mandates. Did you not see that poll?**

**OH REALLY?** O'Reilly was wrong. The poll found that support for going to war without UN mandates was far lower: 37 percent. What was 66 percent? President Bush's approval rating. O'Reilly should have known this—he reported it on Fox the day before.

## ? ? ?

**O'REILLY:** In response to O'Reilly's claim about 66 percent support for war without UN approval, Fertik said, "I also saw the CBS poll which had it the other way around." O'Reilly's response: "No, it didn't."

---

### CORRECTING HIMSELF

**O'REILLY: There isn't one Arab Muslim country supporting us in the war on terror, and I say, Mr. Ambassador, if you don't support us—**

**GUEST: No, that's not true.**

**O'REILLY: Well, Kuwait and Qatar maybe.**

**GUEST: No. Bill—let me talk about the country that I—**

**O'REILLY: Morocco.** (9/10/02)

---

**OH REALLY?** Again, O'Reilly was wrong. The CBS poll showed 52 percent of Americans thought the United States should follow the UN's lead, while 37 percent thought the United States should "decide on its own."

Had enough? O'Reilly sure had, as he quickly finished the interview: "I have seen spinners in my life, but you are at the top of the list. . . . So we are going to bid you adieu. We appreciate you coming in. But it's a No-Spin Zone."

O'Reilly managed to get the last word at the end of the show, after Fertik was safely off-camera: "Earlier in the broadcast, you heard Bob Fertik, the founder of democrats.com, say that a new CBS poll opposed military action in Iraq. I told Mr. Fertik that was not true, and it's not. Here are the poll numbers. When asked by CBS, 'Do you approve or disapprove of the United States taking military action against Iraq to try to remove Saddam Hussein from power?' 68 percent of Americans approved; 26 percent disapproved. Once again, this is a No-Spin Zone. We are not going to tolerate deception by anyone because it is ridiculous, all right?" Unless it's O'Reilly who's being deceptive.

## Toot Your Own Horn

**O'REILLY:** "*The Factor* was the first broadcast outlet to report that accused sniper John Allen Muhammad had an association with the Nation of Islam; that's Farrakhan's group" (10/28/02).

**OH REALLY?** "A report out of Seattle says that John Allen Muhammad actually worked for the Nation of Islam guarding its leader, Louis Farrakhan," reported O'Reilly (10/24/02). But his "exclusive" was exactly the same information reported by *NBC Nightly News* earlier that day: "For the past ten years, Muhammad has worshiped with the Nation of Islam, and published reports say he was a security guard at Louis Farrakhan's Million Man March." O'Reilly wasn't even the first at Fox News to report Muhammad's connection to the Nation of Islam—it was also mentioned that day on *Special Report with Brit Hume* and *The Big Story with John Gibson*, both of which air before *The O'Reilly Factor*.

## I Never Said That

**O'REILLY:** After O'Reilly used the racial slur "Mexican wetbacks" on the air, he tried to rationalize his comments this way: "We were talking about border patrol and the problems they were having; I'm going, 'What's the jargon? What's the jargon? We got *coyotes*, right? *Coyotes* and we got *wetbacks*. Is that what they call them? Is that what they call them?' All right? And the guy goes, 'Yeah. *The wetbacks* are the slang for the people who come over and *the coyotes* are the slang for the people who get paid to bring them over.' That was the context. The next day, 'O'Reilly called Mexicans "wetbacks."' It's an outrage. It's outrageous. They do it all the time, the demonizers, the witch-hunters. They can't argue with you on a policy basis, but if they disagree with you, they try to destroy you. Awful" (CNBC, 4/26/03).

**OH REALLY?** The guest that night, Congressman Silvestre Reyes, had nothing to do with confirming the linguistic origin of O'Reilly's racist slur—O'Reilly did that himself. As transcribed in the Nexis news database, the slur came out of O'Reilly's mouth during a discussion about putting U.S. troops on the border: "We'd save lives because Mexican wetbacks, whatever you want to call them, the coyotes—they're not going to do what they're doing now, all right, so people aren't going to die in the desert." The only thing that Reyes says after that is a response to O'Reilly's statement that "You are in the minority on this one." Reyes said, "Listen, just because we're in the minority doesn't mean we're not right, Bill."

## Fractured History

### DEFENDING THE BOMBING OF HIROSHIMA AND NAGASAKI

 **O'REILLY:** "I wouldn't be here because my father would be dead right now, and 250,000 Americans were estimated to be killed in the invasion of that island" (1/31/03)

**OH REALLY?** The planners of the invasion estimated that in a worst-case scenario, 46,000 U.S. troops would have died, according to declassified 1945 documents from the Joint War Planning Committee (*Bulletin of the Atomic Scientists*, June–July 1986). Higher numbers like those cited by O'Reilly were later put forward by officials involved with the bombing decision, but without documentary evidence. The U.S. invasion force was only scheduled to include 190,000 combat troops (*New York Times*, 1/31/95). It's far from clear that an invasion would have been necessary, even without the atomic bombings. As General Dwight Eisenhower wrote in his memoirs, "My belief [was] that Japan was already defeated and that dropping the bomb was completely unnecessary" (*Mandate for Change*, p. 312).

### FOLLOWING THE TRAIL IN CAMBODIA

**O'REILLY:** When actress and comedian Janeane Garofalo mentioned the Nixon-Kissinger bombing of Cambodia, O'Reilly corrected her: "Our airplanes were bombing the Ho Chi Minh Trail, where North Vietnamese were coming down." When Garofalo asked him, "So we didn't have a secret bombing campaign of Cambodia?" O'Reilly repeated: "Sure we did, on the Ho Chi Minh Trail, Miss Garofalo. That goes through Cambodia" (12/10/02).

**OH REALLY?** The Ho Chi Minh Trail was hardly the only U.S. target in Cambodia. According to William Shawcross's *Sideshow: Kissinger, Nixon, and the Destruction of Cambodia* (Simon and Schuster, 1979), the definitive account of the bombing, in the summer of 1970 "much of the country was a free-fire zone for the United States aircraft." Maps in Shawcross's book show that the United States was directing air strikes throughout the country.

## ? ? ?

**O'REILLY:** O'Reilly has long been an advocate for militarizing the U.S. border with Mexico: "I'd put the army on the border, is what I would—the Treaty of Guadalupe Hidalgo, bang, that's gone." As he elaborated, "We don't need this Treaty of Guadalupe Hidalgo. This is bunch of baloney. The Mexican army is on the border, and they're shooting at us half the time down there. I know I'm overstating a little bit, but you know the problems down on that border" (6/8/00).

**OH REALLY?** Overstating it "a little bit" is right—"half the time" was actually a reference to a single incident near the border town of El Paso, Texas. O'Reilly's claim that the Treaty of Guadalupe Hidalgo—which ended the Mexican-American war in 1848—prevents the United States from placing troops on the border is just wrong: Article XVI of the treaty states: "Each of the contracting parties reserves to itself the entire right to fortify whatever point within its territory it may judge proper so to fortify for its security."

### IRAQ

**O'REILLY:** "Senator |John| Kerry . . . is one of the few people on the Hill who felt that the Gulf War in 1991 could have been handled a little bit differently. He voted against the military action because he wanted more time for Americans to come together about the war and things like that" (5/22/02).

**OH REALLY?** Kerry voted against the resolution authorizing the Gulf War, but he wasn't "one of the few." The Senate vote authorizing the use of force against Iraq was fifty-two to forty-seven (*New York Times*, 1/13/91).

## ? ? ?

 **O'REILLY:** Former *Wall Street Journal* editor Jude Wanniski tried to discuss Gulf War history, making a reference to U.S. officials who were aware of Saddam Hussein's intention to invade Kuwait:

**WANNISKI: And we said we had no complaints about his having a border dispute. It was only after he went into Kuwait that we said—**

**O'REILLY: So your contention is the United States said it was OK for him to invade Kuwait.**

**WANNISKI: We told—Our ambassador, April Glaspie, on the instructions of the State Department—**

**O'REILLY: And what year was that?**

**WANNISKI: That was 1990.**

**O'REILLY: OK, so, see, this is the first time I am hearing of this, and I don't believe that to be true. (7/9/02)**

**OH REALLY?** "We have no opinion on the Arab-Arab conflicts, like your border disagreement with Kuwait," U.S. Ambassador to Iraq April Glaspie told Hussein in July 1990. Glaspie acknowledged that she made the comment (Associated Press, 1/18/92).

## ? ? ?

**O'REILLY:** On January 9, 2003, a caller to O'Reilly's radio show suggested that the U.S. government, thanks to a 1983 meeting between Saddam Hussein and Donald Rumsfeld, had supplied the Iraqi government with chemical and biological weapons. O'Reilly was incensed: "Look, Don, that's been denied by every single federal official in the government. . . . This is another nutty, crazy thing that goes out on the Internet that you guys pick up and think is true."

**OH REALLY?** You don't need to believe in Internet conspiracies to understand the connections between Rumsfeld's 1983 visit with Saddam and subsequent U.S. assistance. Take *Newsweek*'s account: "The meeting between Rumsfeld and Saddam was consequential: for the next five years, until Iran finally capitulated, the United States backed Saddam's armies with military intelligence, economic aid, and covert supplies of munitions" (9/23/02). As the magazine notes, "Over the protest of some Pentagon skeptics, the Reagan administration began allowing the Iraqis to buy a wide variety of 'dual use' equipment and materials from American suppliers. . . . Most unsettling, numerous shipments of 'bacteria/fungi/protozoa' [were made] to the IAEC [Iraq Atomic Energy Commission]. According to former officials, the bacteria cultures could be used to make biological weapons, including anthrax."

## Police Brutality

 **O'REILLY:** Referring to antiwar protests at the beginning of the war with Iraq: "What about the people who cause property damage, and people who hurt the police? In both San Francisco and Chicago, dozens of police officers were injured" (3/24/03).

**OH REALLY?** There were two police injuries reported in San Francisco (*San Francisco Chronicle*, 3/21/03) and none in Chicago.

## Correcting O'Reilly

Sometimes a guest who sticks to the facts provides a valuable service—for at least that one moment, O'Reilly's audience is spared more of his misinformation.

 **O'REILLY:** When O'Reilly claimed that the United States "give[s] far and away more tax money to foreign countries than anyone else. . . . Nobody else even comes close to us" (5/8/01), Phyllis Bennis of the Institute for Policy Studies explained that U.S. contributions per capita were lower than those of any member of the European Union. "That's not true," O'Reilly responded.

**OH REALLY?** According to the Organization for Economic Cooperation and Development, in 2000 the United States gave only 0.1 percent of its Gross National Income as official development aid—less than Italy, the least generous EU nation. Denmark gave ten times as much on a per capita basis. Even in real terms, Japan in 2000 gave away one third more aid, even though its economy was less than half as large.

O'Reilly, perhaps frustrated when Bennis referred to the simple facts, tried to switch gears and spin the numbers his way: "Well, we have a 300 million population base here and Sweden has 3 million, so that's skewed out." The actual Swedish population, although irrelevant, is close to 9 million.

## Admitting He's Wrong

It's not that O'Reilly never admits his errors—on a few occasions, he's done just that. But on the mistake that probably has received the most attention, O'Reilly's record is somewhat mixed.

**O'REILLY:** "More than one hundred thousand abductions of children by strangers every year in the United States. So that's not that rare . . . I mean, if you, if you—there's 365 days in a year, more than a hundred thousand, OK? So we're talking thirty a day? I mean, that's a big number" (7/16/02).

**OH REALLY?** The total number is just *slightly* lower than one hundred thousand. It's about one hundred, according to the Justice Department.

When writer Eric Alterman offered this as a prime example of O'Reilly's inaccurate tendencies, O'Reilly interrupted him: "We corrected that, and that was—that's infamous. . . . we made a mistake, and we corrected it" (2/11/03).

Even that admission is not quite true. The night after making the "hundred thousand" claim, O'Reilly's apparent "correction" was: "Each year in the United States, about a hundred children are abducted by strangers." He never actually indicated that he had made a mistake; but he did correct a different error that night: "Approximately 725,000 are reported missing each year, and many of those cases are not solved. That's a bit under what we reported yesterday, and we're sorry for the error." To make things even more confusing, a month after making his "correction," he wasn't buying the numbers: "I don't believe the statistics. I know that the FBI says a hundred stranger abductions and all of that" (8/27/02).

# Bill O'Reilly, Media Critic

**Well, everywhere else in the world lies. If you see the foreign coverage, it's just a bunch of propaganda.**
**(O'REILLY EXPLAINS FOREIGN PRESS COVERAGE OF IRAQ, 1/17/03)**

**G**iven his many years of experience in the big-time news business, it's not surprising that O'Reilly fancies himself a bit of a media critic. But his "no-spin" analysis hews closely to the tired, familiar conservative script on media bias: the *New York Times* is "primarily a left-wing organization," the *Los Angeles Times* is "the pro-Palestinian newspaper of record out there in L. A.," and National Public Radio provides "a liberal slant . . . twenty-four hours a day."

Just like the professional media critics of the Right, O'Reilly's media analysis has little to do with correcting bad journalism; instead, it's a chance to score political points on the cheap. Consider the following insight, pulled from a discussion between O'Reilly and far-right pundit Ann Coulter: "Now I want to give you an example of something that I've seen that disturbs me. And that's the abortion issue, when it's always framed by the *New York Times* as 'reproductive rights.' . . . That to me is way, way over the line. And they do it all the time . . . I mean, OK, reproductive rights. Fine. Where are the fetuses' rights?"

## Company Man: Defending Fox

Much of O'Reilly's media criticism, in fact, is devoted to fending off critics of his own show, and Fox News Channel in general. Like his Fox costars, the first response to a charge that Fox leans right is to assert that the *real* problem is the rest of the media: "Conservative Americans certainly embraced the News Channel because, let's face it, what are they going to do when you have NPR and when you have other outlets where you can't even hear a conservative point of view?" (*St. Paul Pioneer Press*, 1/29/02)

Of course, the idea that you "can't even hear" conservatives outside of Fox News is beyond absurd—conservatives such as Pat Buchanan and Robert Novak have long had a comfortable perch at CNN; right-wingers dominate talk radio, and they're fixtures on shows like ABC's *Nightline* and PBS's *NewsHour with Jim Lehrer*.

But don't tell that to O'Reilly. In his world, Fox "gives voice to people who can't get on other networks. When was the last time you saw pro-life people [on other networks] unless they shot somebody?" (*Philadelphia Inquirer*, 4/10/01) A question like that is easily answered. In the three years before he made his claim, the National Right to Life Committee's spokespeople had appeared on CNN twenty-one times, compared with sixteen appearances by their pro-choice counterpart, the National Abortion Rights Action League.

Conservatives are plentiful throughout the media but are even more overrepresented on Fox News Channel. When FAIR studied the guest list of the interview segments on Fox's newscast *Special Report with Brit Hume*, the tilt was overwhelming: Of the fifty-six partisan guests on

---

### BALANCING BILL MOYERS ON PBS

**He's being paid partially by taxpayer money. Now if PBS wants to do that, they should have Rush Limbaugh on there, paying him, to have the same kind of balance. Isn't that fair to the taxpayer? Take [Fox host Sean] Hannity. Take anybody. Take any other voice to balance Moyers and give the taxpayer a break. That would be fair, would it not? (1/20/03)**

*Special Report* between January and May 2001, fifty were Republicans and six were Democrats—a greater than eight-to-one imbalance.

On other occasions, O'Reilly runs into trouble trying to cite hard data to back up his claims:

**O'REILLY:** When questioned by NBC's Tim Russert about whether or not he's a conservative, O'Reilly offered this reply: "If you want to think I'm a conservative, go ahead. I mean, our audience is, according to the Pew Research Center, 47 percent Democrat on *The Factor*" (CNBC, 4/26/03).

**OH REALLY:** That's almost the opposite of what the study said. The Pew Research Center actually found that Fox News Channel's audience was 46 percent conservative, 32 percent moderate, and 18 percent liberal (6/9/02). The audience for *The O'Reilly Factor*, though, skewed a bit more to the right: 56 percent of viewers were conservative, while 5 percent identified themselves as liberal. The study did not identify Fox viewers by party affiliation, as O'Reilly claimed.

## NPR: "This Is Personal"

A favorite target of O'Reilly's is NPR—an obsession he describes as "personal, this is absolutely personal. . . . I've had two number-one best sellers. . . . Not one NPR invitation." It's important to note right off the bat that he's spinning: O'Reilly was profiled on the NPR show *On the Media* in January 2001 (more on that one later).

He's not one to take any offense—even an imaginary one—lying down, so he lets NPR have it, attacking the network's "left-wing point of view" (3/6/02):

> **NPR is constant left-wing banging on the drum. . . . It's a left-wing bastion paid for by us. . . . a whole network devoted to putting out the left point of view, the socialistic point of view. . . .**
>
> **What about our pals over at National Public Radio? They have 680 affiliates across the country, and at any given moment, you can hear a pro-Palestinian report, a pro-choice report, and environmentalists put in a favorable light, and on and on. . . . Come on! If you want a liberal slant, it is there on the radio twenty-four hours a day.**

Unfortunately for O'Reilly, such exaggerations are easy to check:

 **O'REILLY:** "I've never heard a right-wing person on NPR anywhere. . . . You never hear a pro-life person on NPR. You never hear an anti–global warming person on NPR. They don't get on there" (1/7/02).

**OH REALLY:** Conservatives, of course, appear regularly on NPR, both in commentary (e.g., *The Weekly Standard*'s David Brooks and the Heritage Foundation's Joe Loconte) and as sources in news stories. Myron Ebell of the Competitive Enterprise Institute, who as a global warming skeptic represents a tiny fraction of the scientific debate, was on NPR three times the previous year; the network quoted Douglas Johnson of the National Right to Life Committee eleven times in 2001.

## Picking on Bush

The *New York Times* isn't much better than NPR in O'Reilly's mind. O'Reilly detected some anti-Bush slant in the *Times* during the 2000 campaign:

**O'REILLY:** "What the *New York Times* did was they did an interview with Governor Bush and it centered on Senator McCain. They ran it on March 16th with this headline. Let's put it up on the screen right now: 'Bush Rebuffs Bid to Embrace Views by McCain'" (3/23/00).

So far, so good. But O'Reilly continues: "So, the next day, on page one again, here's the *Times* headline: 'Bush Makes Effort to Smooth Relations with McCain Camp.' Same interview. Different writers. . . . The strange thing here is that you have two articles on page one with two different headlines culled from the same interview."

**OH REALLY:** That's just wrong. The first article (3/16/00) was based on an interview with Bush. The second article, which ran the following day, was not "culled from the same interview." It was a follow-up article documenting the fallout from the first interview, as the Bush campaign and the McCain people reacted to Bush's

---

### STICKING UP FOR RUSH

**MICHAEL STINSON (Take Back the Media): He's told people to take the bone out of their nose and call him back. Black people. Is that not racist?**

**O'REILLY: He's never said that, and, Mr. Stinson—**

**STINSON: He has said that.**

**O'REILLY: No, he has not.**

**Limbaugh said this to a black caller: "Take that bone out of your nose and call me back." (Newsday, 10/8/90)**

statements. This was obvious by the article's second paragraph, which recounted how "aides and supporters of Mr. McCain criticized Mr. Bush for remarks in an interview with the *New York Times* on Wednesday." The article also mentioned that "in a series of telephone calls yesterday, the Bush camp sought to smooth relations with the McCain camp," and that at one public appearance Bush seemed to refer to the first article, saying, "There's a story out today that doesn't characterize how I feel."

After the socialists at NPR and the left-wing censors at the *New York Times*, the *Los Angeles Times* is probably next on O'Reilly's list of lefty media outlets. During the war in Iraq, he was especially sensitive to the paper's critical reporting of the conflict. But sometimes his charges didn't match reality.

 **O'REILLY:** "Well, today on the front page of the [Los Angeles] *Times*, its management had to apologize because one of its war photographers doctored a picture that also appeared on the front page of the *Times*. The photograph was distorted to make it look like a coalition soldier was pointing his weapon at civilians when, in reality, he was not. The *Los Angeles Times* has fired that photographer, but I'll say it again: There's something very wrong at that newspaper" (4/2/03).

 **OH REALLY:** The photographer had combined two similar images into one photo—a definite no-no—and was fired. But the effect did not make it look like the soldier was "pointing his weapon at civilians." The photo was altered to make it appear as if

there were more civilians in the frame; as the *Los Angeles Times* explained in the editor's note that O'Reilly may have missed, "several civilians in the background appear twice." Nothing about the soldier's weapon, or where it was pointed, was altered.

On February 24, 1999, O'Reilly's "Most Ridiculous Item of the Day" was dedicated to the *Los Angeles Times*. That night, NBC was scheduled to air its interview with Juanita Broaddrick, a woman who accused Bill Clinton of raping her in 1978.

 **O'REILLY:** "If you want to understand why President Clinton is so popular here in Southern California, look no further than the *Los Angeles Times*. L. A.'s only major newspaper has reported not one word of the Juanita Broaddrick story. Not one word" (2/24/99).

**OH REALLY:** The *Times* had run a short story about Broaddrick's allegations on February 20. With no way to confirm or rebut her charges, most media outlets were unable to report much about the case, especially prior to the NBC interview.

Two years later, O'Reilly was still telling the same story, which at that point was even further from the truth. In a profile in *MediaWeek*, O'Reilly declared that the *Los Angeles Times* "never mentioned Juanita Broaddrick's name, ever. This whole area out here has no idea what's going on, unless you watch my show" (2/8/01). As former *Los Angeles Times* editor Melissa Payton pointed out to *MediaWeek*, the paper's on-line archive contained twenty-one citations of Broaddrick's name.

## Breaking the Story

What steams O'Reilly the most is media outlets that don't share his news values. In the midst of his coverage of a pornographic movie surrepti-

tiously shot inside an Indiana University dorm room, O'Reilly chided the local media for not being appropriately outraged.

**O'REILLY:** "The *Indianapolis Star* has simply been MIA in the dorm porn scandal" (12/6/02).

**OH REALLY:** While the *Star* (a paper owned by Dan Quayle's family) may not have thought the story was as important as O'Reilly did, they weren't MIA. They reported on the dormitory high jinks on October 24, 2002. O'Reilly's first report on the subject aired almost a month later, on November 15.

## International Watchdog

O'Reilly doesn't confine his media criticism to U.S. outlets. On April 2, 2003, he took a shot at the Arab satellite channel Al Jazeera.

**O'REILLY:** "I've got a transcript of what they do and a rundown of their whole lineup. And look, twenty-five years Saddam has been committing atrocities, all right? Al Jazeera didn't report on them. They didn't report on the mow-downs after the '91 war. They didn't report on the gassing of the Kurds in the eighties."

**OH REALLY:** As his guest helpfully pointed out, it would have been difficult for Al Jazeera to report on Iraq in the eighties, or even during the Gulf War: the channel was founded in 1996. O'Reilly offered a weak response: "No, but there's a lot of file footage available to run now."

The British Broadcasting Corporation (BBC) was also nailed for skewing its coverage against the 2003 war in Iraq. When the Saddam Hussein statue was pulled down in Baghdad, O'Reilly claimed that the BBC didn't cover it:

**O'REILLY:** (to Newt Gingrich): "Did you know—did you know, Mr. Speaker, that the BBC didn't run the statue, cut away to an earthquake in India instead of running the most visual moment in the last ten years, the BBC?" (4/9/03)

O'Reilly later repeated the charge: "They've been disgraceful in their war coverage, as we mentioned. Just today, as I said, instead of showing a Saddam statue coming down, they covered an earthquake in India."

**OH REALLY:** If you think it's unlikely that the BBC somehow ignored the most famous image of the war, you're right. Two days later, O'Reilly made a rare apology: "I may owe the BBC an apology. Some of their services were slow to show the statue, but their primary ones were on the story. BBC still did a terrible job covering this war, but I owe them an apology. I gave a blanket statement, and I was wrong there."

## Seeing Is Believing

Watching the media he criticizes seems almost irrelevant to O'Reilly's ability to speak with confidence. When O'Reilly interviewed Hussam Akkawi of Qatar TV, he made it clear that while the segment would address Arab media's coverage of the Iraq war, "I haven't seen your network, and I don't think you're nearly as bad as Al Jazeera" (4/3/03). When O'Reilly told Akkawi that "you are reporting the facts straight now, and we're glad of that," Akkawi protested, "We have been always been, Bill. We have been always doing this."

O'Reilly's confident rebuttal came in triplicate: "No way. No way. No way. But that's all right. We'll have a gentlemen's disagreement, OK? But, Al Jazeera and your network and all of that have been sympathetic to the Iraqi point of view. Would you not agree with that? You've been sympathetic to their point of view?" Wait a second—didn't O'Reilly just finish saying he'd never seen Qatar TV?

The war in Iraq provided a clear contrast between the elite media O'Reilly so despises and the reporting on, say, Fox News. Even after the shooting largely stopped, O'Reilly was still peeved. Not all of the media are peddling far-left war stories, though; though he had been critical of their coverage, O'Reilly singled out a piece in the *New York Times* by Judith Miller: "It's also important to note that reporter Judith Miller of the *New York Times* does believe the weapons are there. She spelled out the weapons yesterday" (4/22/03). Miller's piece did not "spell out" any weapons, though. Her report alleged, based on secondhand information she was not allowed to verify, that an Iraqi scientist had located some sites where chemical precursors—not weapons—were buried. In fact, the unnamed Iraqi source claimed that weapons were actually destroyed prior to the war. But who's counting.

# O'Reilly Plays the Numbers

## I RESEARCH UP THE WAZOO. (5/4/00)

**T**he *O'Reilly Factor* is hardly the place to go If you're looking for actual "news" or original reporting. This seems to be by design. Strong and loud opinions dominate the broadcast, with occasional unverifiable factoids thrown in for good measure.

So when O'Reilly injects some hard numbers into his questions and commentaries, it pays to be skeptical. The numbers are usually just trotted out to confirm O'Reilly's opinions. O'Reilly's generalizations about drug abuse among the homeless were apparently supported by this wandering phrase: "We have brand new research here from the Urban Institute, 70 percent are addicted or mentally ill or whatever" (12/19/02).

"Or whatever" is a bit better than some other nights, when O'Reilly sounds as if he's simply making it up as he goes along.

Of course, it's not dishonest for a commentator to cite specific numbers just to confirm his opinions on a subject. But sometimes O'Reilly is citing research that has been seriously challenged, without giving viewers any sense that what they're hearing is anything but the unvarnished truth.

97

# One of These Is Right

During an interview with National Organization for Women President Kim Gandy, O'Reilly claimed that "58 percent of single-mom homes are on welfare" (2/5/02). When Gandy questioned that figure, O'Reilly held firm: "You can't say no, Miss Gandy. That's the stat. You can't just dismiss it. . . . It's 58 percent. That's what it is from the federal government."

Gandy, to her credit, didn't buy it. So, by the next broadcast, O'Reilly had revised his accounting: "At this point, we have this from Washington, and it's bad. Fifty-two percent of families receiving public assistance are headed by a single mother—52 percent" (2/6/02). Bad for who—those on public assistance, or for O'Reilly? Not only is that a different number, it's the reverse of the statistic he offered the previous night—not the percentage of households headed by single mothers that receive welfare, but the percentage of families receiving public assistance headed by single mothers. That's a distinction that O'Reilly did not attempt to clarify; he seemed unapologetic about emphatically putting forward an unsupported statistic the night before.

But the confusion didn't end there. The following night, O'Reilly came up with more solid figures, but they bore no resemblance to his original numbers: About 14 percent of single mothers receive federal welfare benefits, he now said—less than one-fourth of his earlier claim. (He suggested that food stamps ought to be considered a kind of welfare, but that only gets him to 33 percent—still 25 percentage points short.) O'Reilly explained that "it's really hard to get a stat to say how many single moms percentagewise get government assistance" (2/7/02). Funny, he'd found it easy enough to pull one out of the air just three nights earlier.

Mix welfare and drug abuse, and you've got something O'Reilly can really go after. The idea of welfare recipients buying drugs with O'Reilly's tax money gets him worked up, and he's ready to get to the bottom of it. It started with O'Reilly claiming that a study from Columbia University's

Center for Addiction and Substance Abuse found that "20 percent" of "welfare recipients are using drugs, U.S. Department of Health and Human Services estimates 15 percent" (10/20/99).

The 20 percent figure might be correct; the National Household Survey of Drug Abuse from 1994 and 1995 found that about 20 percent of welfare recipients reported using illegal drugs in the previous year (*Journal of Health Politics, Policy, and Law*, August 2000).

Interviewing the president of the Center for Addiction and Substance Abuse, Joseph Califano, O'Reilly put the numbers this way: "About 25 percent of welfare recipients surveyed admit they use illegal drugs" (9/19/02).

O'Reilly's numbers increased again about a month later, when he claimed that "every study shows between 30 percent to 50 percent of people on government assistance are using drugs" (10/28/02). When his guest questioned that claim, O'Reilly was incredulous: "All right. Look, Columbia University is crazy then, all right? Columbia University is nuts. All of their research—we'll throw it right out the window, right?" By that time, *Factor* viewers had already heard him cite three different statistics for drug use among welfare recipients, and none of them fell into the range O'Reilly claimed as the parameters of "every study" on the topic.

## That Sounds Right: Illegal Immigration

O'Reilly has a favorite number for the cost of undocumented immigration:

> **It is estimated by Rice University that undocumented aliens cost U.S. taxpayers $24 billion every year. (6/18/02)**

> **American taxpayers are forking out $24 billion every year to pay for health benefits and other subsidies for illegal immigrants. (6/20/02)**

O'Reilly is referring to a 1997 American Immigration Control Foundation report, *Public Costs of Immigration*, prepared by Donald Huddle, an update of research Huddle did in 1993. The General Accounting Office (GAO) studied Huddle's work in 1995 and found that his study was marred by serious errors. For starters, he includes costs such as unemployment compensation and student financial aid, both of which undocumented immigrants are ineligible to receive. The GAO also found that Huddle double-counted some costs and made at least one arithmetic error. Also, his calculation for job displacement—the work opportunities that undocumented immigrants take away from citizens—is "inconsistent with research findings on this topic."

So why does O'Reilly cite one figure so often, instead of giving a range that better reflects the debate? Because he's more interested in clutching at any statistic that will conform to his opinion on the subject. "The stat is in stone: 30 percent of Mexican immigrants are on the dole here," O'Reilly claimed on one show (1/9/03). When one of his guests challenged him, O'Reilly briefly engaged the argument with one of his favorite comebacks—"Well, look, madam, if you want to live in the land of Oz, you go ahead." Then he cut off her microphone and apologized to his audience: "The woman has no idea what she's talking about, and I'm sorry to impose her on the international audience. The 30 percent comes from the Center for Immigration Studies. It is a true statistic, and—whatever."

The idea that the research put out by an anti-immigration group like the Center for Immigration Studies could be questioned wasn't even permissible. Perhaps some day one of O'Reilly's guests could challenge the stats—providing that he would keep their microphone on.

# Going Nuclear

**O'REILLY:** When John Passacantando of Greenpeace argued that nuclear power is "the most uneconomic form of energy in the world today," O'Reilly stopped him cold. "Hold it—No-Spin Zone," O'Reilly said. "You just made a flat-out statement, the most uneconomical power in the world today. Here we go. The Utility Data Institute did a study in 1999. Nuclear energy had an average production cost of $1.83 per kilowatt-hour; natural gas, $3.52 per kilowatt-hour. Once again, nuclear energy, $1.83; natural gas, which is what we're using in California and many other states, $3.52. So, that's flat-out wrong, what you just said" (5/1/01).

**OH REALLY:** For starters, all those numbers should be *cents* per kilowatt-hour, not dollars. But energy economics are about more than just the production costs at the plant; O'Reilly is giving a badly limited view of the true costs. Even the Nuclear Energy Institute (NEI) is more honest about the real costs. In a press release heralding the arrival of the numbers O'Reilly was citing, the group noted that "production costs do not represent the complete cost of electricity at nuclear power plants" (NEI news release, 1/9/01). The reason? The public picks up the other, unmentioned costs associated with nuclear power, including the capital costs of building the plants—or cleaning up after them (see FAIR's magazine *Extra!* for July–August 2001).

## I Don't Like Your Stats

O'Reilly frequently refuses to believe some of his guests—even when they support their arguments with data. That's especially true if he just so happens to not like the fact being cited. When one *Factor* interviewee

remarked that "60 percent of all people will live in poverty for one year of their life," O'Reilly shot back, "Not in the United States. . . . No, that's bogus. I mean, that's a socialist stat. You can believe it if you want to, but it's not true" (3/1/02).

A socialist stat? When the guest explained that the number comes from research at Cornell University, O'Reilly dismissed it: "Well, what more do I have to say?"—as if any information coming from an Ivy League institution had to be wrong.

When Keith Stroup of the National Organization for the Reform of Marijuana Laws argued that the rate of marijuana usage in Holland, where it's legal, is lower than it is in the United States, O'Reilly wasn't about to believe that kind of nonsense: "Well, that's skewed out because their population is so much less" (5/1/02).

Stroup explained that he was referring to percentages, so O'Reilly simply changed course, arguing that the Dutch government cannot be trusted: "That statistic's skewed. And the government won't tell you— if you go over and ask the government of the Netherlands to tell us about how many kids get caught, they won't tell you. I don't believe them for a second."

## What the Numbers Mean

O'Reilly can be quite fond of a statistic, however, when he thinks it makes a point for him. "Here's the statistic that tells me American society and the system we have in place works for both blacks and whites," he told Walter Fields, former NAACP political director in New Jersey (5/15/01). "Eighty percent, all right, 80 percent of what whites earn, blacks earn if they stay together in a committed relationship, whether it's marriage or living together. So if a black man and woman are married and stay together, they earn 80 percent of what white couples earn. And the reason it isn't 100 percent is because more blacks live in the

102

South, where the salaries are lower. That tells me that the American system, the capitalistic system, works and is fair. Where it's broken down—all right, you may disagree with that, but that stat is rock solid."

O'Reilly's idea that blacks overall are poorer because they have chosen not to marry doesn't hold water. Black single mothers earn only 65 percent of what white single mothers do, even though they have the same family structure. And the notion that living in the South explains blacks' lower incomes is a fantasy. Blacks in the South, according to the U.S. Census Bureau, actually make more money than blacks in the Northeast.

What's most telling about O'Reilly's argument is what the statistics mean to him. When asked to comment on the 80 percent stat, Walter Fields said what any reasonable person might: "I don't consider a 20 percent differential almost parity." O'Reilly's response: "All right. I do." The fact that O'Reilly finds equality in such disparity speaks volumes.

# O'Reilly vs. O'Reilly

**I'm a linear thinker. I was educated in that way. I have a master's degree from Harvard in public policy.** (O'REILLY ON NPR, 7/30/02)

**S**ometimes, you don't have to contrast O'Reilly's comments with reality—you can just compare them to other things that he has said.

## What Would Jesus Do?

**O'REILLY:** "Both sides of the debate are saying God is on their side. Those who favor peace point to the pope calling the war immoral, and those who favor the removal of an evil man, Saddam, say they're protecting lives by that action. In this case, I think both sides are wrong. Nobody knows for sure what the absolute right thing to do is. We can only have opinions. Thus, it's intellectually dishonest to be claiming God is on your side when only God knows for sure what the right thing to do is" (3/11/03).

**VS. O'REILLY:** "I'm telling you, I'm telling you that President Bush is doing just what Jesus would have done" (12/4/02).

## Things I'll Never Say

**O'REILLY:** "Now I feel sorry for Jackson's wife and kids, especially for the baby. I will not comment on his personal behavior" (1/19/01).

**VS. O'REILLY:** O'Reilly explained to *Newsweek* magazine that his daughter was the "same age as Jesse Jackson's. Only she's legitimate" (2/12/01).

**O'REILLY:** "I've done this program for four and a half years, and I have never attacked anybody personally on this program ever" (3/13/01).

**VS. O'REILLY:** About Monica Lewinsky: "She's got the IQ of a tomato!" (1/21/99)

Before the passage of Bush's dividend tax cut:

**O'REILLY:** Referring to President Bush: "What if he says, 'I'm going to cut the dividend, because I believe if I cut the dividend tax, and O'Reilly, who's sitting on some money, is going to buy more stock and that's going to stimulate business so more jobs are created'? Come on, that makes economic sense. You might not agree with it, but it makes sense. . . . Investment in big business expands big business" (1/28/03).

After the tax cut passed:

**VS. O'REILLY:** Congress has approved a tax cut. Nobody really knows if it will stimulate the economy" (5/22/03).

## Evolving on Sharpton

**O'REILLY:** "Al Sharpton is probably the most dangerous person that African Americans have to deal with. . . . I can't stand Al Sharpton, and I think Congressman [Gregory] Meeks denigrates himself by sticking up for Sharpton who, to me, represents the worst of American society" (6/22/99).

**VS. O'REILLY:** "Look, do I think Sharpton's a bad man? No, I don't" (CNBC, 4/26/03).

## O'Reilly for Socialism?

**ROBERT REICH** (former secretary of labor): "Why not exempt the first $7,000 of your income from payroll taxes? Most Americans, as you know, pay more in payroll taxes than they do in income taxes. . . . And so why not exempt the first $7,000 whether you are making $5 million a year or you're making $20,000 a year, . . ."

**O'REILLY:** "All right, yeah. . . . Fine, I'm for that" (1/17/01).

**VS. O'REILLY:** "But look, Robert Reich, you know him? He borders on socialism sometimes, he wants to say the first $7,000 in Social Security payments, payroll tax, nobody pays" (1/23/01).

**VS. O'REILLY:** "I agree with you that I would cut the payroll taxes for Social Security" (interviewing Reich again, 11/12/02).

## Killing Civilians

**O'REILLY:** On bombing Serbia: "Rather than put ground forces at risk where we're going to see five thousand Americans dead, I would rather destroy their infrastructure, totally destroy it. Any target is OK. I'd warn the people, just as we did with Japan, that it's coming, you've got to get out of there, OK, but I would level that country so that there would be nothing moving—no cars, no trains, nothing" (4/26/99).

**VS. O'REILLY:** "No civilized society attacks civilians" (3/27/02).

## Which Constitution?

**O'REILLY:** "The United States was founded on Judeo-Christian principles and the Founders framed the Constitution around God-given rights" (column, 7/3/02).

**VS. O'REILLY:** "The Founding Fathers took great pains to keep the laws of our country secular so that all beliefs and behavior, legal behavior, would be tolerated" (10/4/02).

## The Economy—Blame Someone (or No One)

**O'REILLY:** "Now millions of Americans are losing their jobs. Why did Alan Greenspan and Bill Clinton allow this to happen?" (1/31/01)

**VS. O'REILLY:** "No government can make the economy better. You know that" (11/12/02).

108

## Too Much Smart?

To O'Reilly, there had been far too much media attention paid to a missing Utah girl named Elizabeth Smart. He commented on his July 11, 2002, broadcast that CNN's Larry King had "seized upon this story and broadcast hours of endless speculation on his CNN program." As O'Reilly opined, "I watched just a few minutes of that and became angry. Mr. King is exploiting this young girl's tragedy for ratings, and he's doing pretty well with it." O'Reilly's words of advice: "The media should not be exploiting the kidnapping of Elizabeth Smart."

Shortly after delivering his sermon, O'Reilly did his fifteenth segment on—you guessed it—*the Elizabeth Smart case.*

## Boycotting Boycotts

Given O'Reilly's incessant pestering of Jesse Jackson, it might come as no surprise that one of Jackson's tactics—high-profile boycotts—might rub O'Reilly the wrong way.

To Al Sharpton: "But I'm just saying to you, it looks to me like a boycott is, number one, un-American. I don't believe in it. Number two, hurts entry-level kids trying to get some discipline in their lives and a start" (12/29/00).

**"Boycotting, I don't think, is American" (12/29/00).**

Speaking about critics of Dr. Laura Schlessinger boycotting her short-lived television show: "This is blatant censorship. And you know who's real happy about this? The gay activists whose—who are gaining more and more power in this society to shut down opinion they don't like, they don't agree with" (5/18/00).

To Michael Stinson, who advocated a boycott of Rush Limbaugh's advertisers: "You don't want him to speak. . . . You're against his freedom of speech" (2/3/03).

It's perfectly reasonable to criticize boycotts as a lever for social or political change. And O'Reilly's position would all be fine and dandy, as long as no one happened to notice that O'Reilly constantly threatens to boycott all sorts of things—including entire countries. A sampling:

## CHINA

When the crew of a U.S. spy plane was held in Chinese custody:

> **I will now officially sanction it. I am not buying any Chinese goods until our people are released. (4/4/01)**

> **I'm boycotting Chinese goods myself. . . . If all three hundred million Americans did that, there would be some big, big trouble in the land of the Asian tiger. (4/6/01)**

## THE AMERICAN RED CROSS

> **I'm officially boycotting the Red Cross until they change their national leadership and their attitude. (3/13/02)**

## FRANCE

Speaking of French help in prosecuting terror suspect Zacarias Moussaoui:

> **I'll tell you what. If you were to withdraw your cooperation now, I would call for a national boycott of France. And I would say that no American should ever go there. (3/21/02)**

## CANADA

> **If they don't play ball, I'm going to call for a boycott of any tourism going to Canada. (6/6/02)**

**If Canada doesn't shape up, we may have to call for a boycott. (6/11/02)**

## MEDIA OUTLETS

After cable channel VH1 aired a show about music programs in prison, and the *Pittsburgh Post-Gazette* endorsed its right to do so: "VH1 and the *Pittsburgh Post-Gazette*, in my opinion, are harming the families of the murder victims. And if I can't get angry about that, then I can't get angry about anything. So far, tens of thousands of you have deleted VH1 from your TV sets, and almost every sponsor has bailed. We're right on this one. VH1 will never recover from this atrocity, and the *Pittsburgh Post-Gazette* should be ashamed of itself" (11/14/02).

## LUDACRIS . . . OR LUDICROUS?

What would seem to be an obvious and obnoxious double standard nearly caught up with O'Reilly when he launched a boycott of Pepsi-Cola after the company chose rapper Ludacris as a commercial spokesperson. To O'Reilly, the rapper's graphic lyrics made him an unacceptable choice to market sugary beverages to impressionable youth. O'Reilly went to work—and got fast results.

> **I'm calling for all responsible Americans to fight back and punish Pepsi for using a man who degrades women, who encourages substance abuse, and does all the things that hurt particularly the poor in our society. I'm calling for all Americans to say, "Hey, Pepsi, I'm not drinking your stuff. You want to hang around with Ludacris, you do that, I'm not hanging around with you." (8/27/02)**

It wasn't long before Pepsi pulled the plug on the Ludacris deal. That left O'Reilly and his army of viewers victorious. Let the celebration begin:

> **Because of pressure by Factor viewers, Pepsi-Cola late today capitulated. Ludacris has been fired. (8/28/02)**

> **And I say this to Ludacris: You have freedom of speech, but I have freedom of association. And anybody that hangs around with you and your ilk, not somebody I'm going to do business with. If all Americans would apply those standards to America's companies, things would change fast in this country. Good guys won a big one this week. Let's keep on rolling. (8/29/02)**

> **The reason that Pepsi reversed itself is that thousands of Americans e-mailed the company and said they would not buy its products as long as Ludacris was endorsing them. The power of the people prevailed. Let's hope a trend has started here. (column, 8/31/02)**

So what was this "pressure," this "trend" that O'Reilly hoped to start? Call it what you will—just don't call it a boycott:

> **I did not call for a boycott of Pepsi. I just said I wouldn't drink it. But now the company has done the right thing. All is well. (9/30/02)**

That's not only false—it's bizarre. As O'Reilly put it in one of his columns, "I'm the guy that started the situation" (9/12/02). Why would someone gloat over a triumph, but then back away from responsibility? After O'Reilly criticized the boycott against Rush Limbaugh, a viewer wrote to question this strange double standard. O'Reilly's response: "I simply said I wasn't going to drink Pepsi while [Ludacris] was on their payroll. No boycott was ever mentioned by me" (2/3/03). Viewers who were keeping score—especially those "responsible Americans" who "won a big one" by following O'Reilly's lead and getting Ludacris booted—must have been a bit confused.

# The World Against Bill

**There is a concerted effort, I believe—and I'm not a paranoid guy, I'm not a conspiracy kind of guy— in some areas of the elite media they don't want you to know about the Factor book.** (10/6/00)

If there's one subject that is examined in excruciating detail on *The O'Reilly Factor*, it's Bill O'Reilly. Responding to each and every criticism launched against our "humble correspondent" has become a semiregular feature of the show. Virtually no criticism goes unreported. Entire segments are fashioned out of the slightest negative press attention.

O'Reilly was outraged at writer Bruce Kluger, who appeared on the show to defend a piece he had written about O'Reilly in *USA Today*. The fact that Kluger dared to write about O'Reilly was bad enough. That *USA Today* would publish it made the whole affair almost unbearable: "Why would *USA Today* print a hit piece like this without asking me to respond?" O'Reilly demanded (1/30/03), an odd suggestion for an op-ed page. "What is not fine is Kluger's agenda running in *USA Today* without challenge. That is cheap and sleazy, and the newspaper should be ashamed."

After appearing on the *Factor*, Kluger wrote about the experience for the *Los Angeles Times*. That was too much for O'Reilly, who steamed:

113

"The *L. A. Times* ran the most vicious hit piece I've ever seen in a major American newspaper. It's full of lies and distortions about us."

You'd think that O'Reilly might have mentioned at least one of the "lies" this "vicious hit piece" was filled with, but he never did. Perhaps the assault on O'Reilly's honor would be too much for some viewers to take. It's more likely that O'Reilly was upset because his on-air slur about "wetbacks" made it into the lead paragraph. Pretty vicious stuff indeed.

But the *Los Angeles Times* and *USA Today* aren't the only newspapers out to get him:

 **O'REILLY:** "The *Orange County Register* dropped my column because I was in favor of the war, and they dropped it. And I thought that was a good example of a paper that, you know, really fears freedom of speech" (3/19/03).

**OH REALLY:** Actually, as the paper's editorial director, Cathy Taylor, pointed out, the *Register* hadn't run O'Reilly's column since August 2002, so it's doubtful that his position on the war got him booted. Instead, Taylor wrote, it was a matter of O'Reilly overload: "The columns were more and more about Bill O'Reilly and Bill O'Reilly's television show and what happened to Bill O'Reilly on Bill O'Reilly's television show. In short, all about Bill" (3/30/03). Taylor reminded readers that the paper's regular roster of columnists still leaned right—folks like William Safire, Thomas Sowell, William F. Buckley, Michelle Malkin, and Walter Williams, to name a few. Not exactly a peace march on the paper's op-ed page.

So would the paper really silence a columnist for backing the war? Hardly. As the *Orange County Weekly*'s R. Scott Moxley put it, "If the *Register* was really against publishing prowar opinions, why has it repeatedly done so? Can a man who has a national television show, a national

radio show, a national syndicated column, a best-selling book, a newsletter, and a website honestly charge that his First Amendment rights have been shortchanged?" (4/11/03) O'Reilly didn't bring up the *Register* brouhaha after the paper set the record straight.

## Shut Out at NPR

The same can be said for O'Reilly's persistent attacks on National Public Radio. "This is personal, this is absolutely personal," he said on January 7, 2002. "I've had two number-one best sellers. . . . Not one NPR invitation." So had O'Reilly really been blacklisted at NPR? Nope. In fact, he'd been profiled on NPR's *On the Media* in January 2001. Tired of hearing about NPR's supposed campaign to exclude O'Reilly from the air waves, the show's senior producer, Arun Rath, finally wrote the following e-mail to O'Reilly, with the subject line "your fantasy world":

> Bill, I'm sick of hearing you say you can't get on NPR. Our own Mike Pesca reported a long piece all about you last year, although you later denied ever hearing of him (odd that you spoke with him over an hour on tape, had him in your office and around while you were taping, and later developed amnesia) AND you've turned down the requests to be on our show since then. We would still love to have you on OTM. Your claim that you can't get on NPR is self-serving bull. So put your money where your mouth is or shut up.
>
> Awaiting your response,
>
> Arun Rath
> Senior Producer, NPR's *On the Media*
> WNYC

One can only hope O'Reilly's regular viewers were comforted by his subsequent appearance on NPR's *Talk of the Nation* (7/30/02). If the whole drama was just a calculated attempt to get airtime on NPR, it worked like a charm.

## Furious Spinning: O'Reilly and the Koran

Before the 2002 fall semester began, incoming freshmen at the University of North Carolina were to be required to read Michael Anthony Sells's book *Approaching the Qu'ran: The Early Revelations*. From O'Reilly's perspective, the angle must have seemed obvious and irresistible: a public school was indoctrinating freshmen in Islamic teachings. So O'Reilly brought on UNC professor Dr. Robert Kirkpatrick to talk about the controversy. Comments O'Reilly made during the interview elicited some pretty serious criticism. O'Reilly, of course, was defensive: "Some Muslim websites wrote that I compared *Mein Kampf* to the Koran. Isn't that nice? Talk about dishonest spin" (8/8/02).

Who's being dishonest? Here's the passage from that interview (7/10/02):

**O'REILLY: But I don't know what this serves to take a look at our enemy's religion. See, I mean, I wouldn't give people a book during World War II on how the emperor was God in Japan. Would you?**

**KIRKPATRICK: Sure, why not? Wouldn't that have explained kamikaze pilots?**

**O'REILLY: No. It would have just—I don't think it would have. I mean, I would say the culture of Japan, fine, but not the religion. The religion aspect of this bothers me. I wouldn't read the book. And I'll tell you why: I wouldn't have read Mein**

Kampf either. If I were going to UNC in 1941 and you, professor, said, "Read Mein Kampf," I would have said, "Hey, professor, with all due respect, shove it. I ain't reading it."

KIRKPATRICK: Why? Well, is that because you think you would have been converted to—if you read it?

O'REILLY: No. It's because it's tripe. Tripe.

It's hard to see how his critics were being dishonest. But O'Reilly fired away at any media outlet that reported on the story: "[ABC] *Nightline* is taking shots at me as well as the *Washington Post*," O'Reilly complained (8/26/02). He went on to spin the interview this way: "The professor claims that knowing about the Koran helps put the terror of 9/11 in perspective. I disagree. The Koran has nothing to do with the war on terror. The criminals that attacked us can hide behind anything they want, in this case religion, but you don't have to understand Islam to understand murder. The two are not joined together. What Professor Kirkpatrick and the elite media want is for Americans to take a sympathetic view of Islam, and that is the agenda in play here."

If O'Reilly were taking freshman English composition, he might get points for creativity. Kirkpatrick never said anything resembling what O'Reilly attributed to him ("knowing about the Koran helps put the terror of 9/11 in perspective"). And while O'Reilly might suggest that the Koran has "nothing to do with the war on terror," that wasn't his position during the interview: "I'm telling you, these are our enemies now. I mean, Islamic fundamentalism is our enemy."

## Warmonger?

Others media figures have taken "shots" at O'Reilly too. Journalist and commentator Bill Moyers was singled out for having the sheer audacity

to say a few words about O'Reilly's suggested response to the September 11 attacks.

**O'REILLY:** "A few days after 9/11, for example, [Bill] Moyers actually attacked me in a speech he gave in Albany, New York. He called me a warmonger because I was calling for an attack on the Taliban government in Afghanistan" (11/12/02).

**OH REALLY:** As he explained in an advertisement in the *New York Daily News*, Moyers never called O'Reilly a warmonger—though if he had, that would have been far too mild. The comments O'Reilly made on September 17, 2001, were the subject of a brief mention in Moyers's speech. An "attack on the Taliban government" was only part of O'Reilly's plan, though; he actually called for the United States to "bomb the Afghan infrastructure to rubble—the airport, the power plants, their water facilities, and the roads. . . . Remember, the people of any country are ultimately responsible for the government they have. The Germans were responsible for Hitler. The Afghans are responsible for the Taliban. We should not target civilians. But if they don't rise up against this criminal government, they starve, period." O'Reilly was just warming up—Iraq would also feel our wrath: "Their infrastructure must be destroyed and the population made to endure yet another round of intense pain." He closed with a warning that the United States should destroy Libya's airports and mine its harbors: "Let them eat sand."

Moyers did not need to call O'Reilly anything at all—the words speak for themselves. Or do they? On his September 25 show, when guest Phil Donahue called him on this bloodthirsty plan, O'Reilly denied ever threatening civilians: "I never said bomb a civilian. I would bomb military targets. . . . I'm not talking about civilians." Perhaps when he hoped Libyans might be forced to "eat sand," he was referring only to Libyan soldiers.

# O'Reilly's Roots

**I'm amused to see how fashionable it has become for the powerful to exaggerate their humble roots.**
**(O'REILLY, WRITING IN NEWSWEEK IN 1987)**

**P**art of the charm of Bill O'Reilly's show is his working-class background. His readers and viewers are constantly reminded that O'Reilly came up the hard way, from populist roots. Even with his media success, O'Reilly asserts that his kind is still not welcome in elite circles. "I've never been invited to an A-list party in my life, basically because I won't kiss anybody's butt, which is what those people desire above all else," O'Reilly once explained (7/26/99). "When I come into any restaurant—I mean, the crosses come out like this, like Dracula."

His book's dust-jacket bio begins: "Bill O'Reilly rose from humble beginnings to become a nationally known broadcast journalist," and O'Reilly says his father, who retired in 1978, "never earned more than $35,000 a year in his life." But others were less impressed with O'Reilly's biography. Editor Michael Kinsley of www.slate.com infuriated O'Reilly by suggesting that the Fox host's background was less proletarian than he was letting on and was actually comfortably middle-class (*Washington Post*, 3/1/01).

As Kinsley pointed out, O'Reilly's father's $35,000 income in 1978 is equivalent to over $90,000 today in inflation-adjusted dollars. Kinsley's column also charged O'Reilly with fabricating a story about being shunned at a tony Washington, D.C., social event because of his working-class roots. The brouhaha only escalated when Kinsley made an ill-advised appearance on *The O'Reilly Factor* (3/20/01).

While O'Reilly makes much of his Levittown roots, his mother told a *Washington Post* reporter that her son actually grew up in Westbury, Long Island, a "middle-class suburb a few miles from Levittown," where he attended private school (*Washington Post*, 12/13/00).

> "O'Reilly's insistence that he's an outsider isn't an affectation; it's a delusion."
> (Noam Scheiber, *The New Republic*, 6/25/01)

Deceptive? Perhaps. But once you hear O'Reilly explain it, things get more confusing. It was "the Westbury section of Levittown," O'Reilly explained to Long Island's *Newsday* (10/18/00). "For the sake of the national audience, I say 'Levittown,' 'cause I lived in a Levitt house, but it's the Westbury post office." Whatever the case, the message is always the same: "I was in with a bunch of Garden City rich kids, and the culture gap was huge. I had one sport jacket from Modell's; they had six sport jackets from Saks. And they made fun of my one sport jacket from Modell's, and I punched them in the mouth" (*Newsday*, 10/16/00).

Other details of O'Reilly's background were similarly scrutinized. O'Reilly's book claims that the no-frills host drives a used car. But as the *Post*'s Paul Farhi pointed out, the "used car" just happened to be a Lexus. O'Reilly now seems to know a little better, even catching himself in mid-exaggeration: "I have a little Honda . . . well, not really. But I have a sedan, all right, just a small sedan" (1/27/03).

## Tabloid Awards

In February 2001, O'Reilly gave a speech seemingly taking credit for winning a coveted Peabody Award while an anchor at *Inside Edition*. Puzzled over which report could have been deserving of such professional accolades, comedian Al Franken decided to dig around for evidence that the show actually snagged a Peabody. He came up empty and explained the tale to the *Washington Post*'s Lloyd Grove. Nonetheless, O'Reilly retorted, in Mametesque syntax: "Guy says about me, couple of weeks ago, 'O'Reilly said he won a Peabody Award.' Never said it. You can't find a transcript where I said it" (3/13/01).

But Franken had. On his May 19, 2000, broadcast, O'Reilly repeatedly told a guest who brought up his tabloid past, "We won Peabody Awards. . . . We won Peabody Awards. . . . A program that wins a Peabody Award, the highest award in journalism, and you're going to denigrate it?"

To be fair, *Inside Edition* did win a Polk Award, not the better-known Peabody—*after* O'Reilly left the show (*Washington Post*, 3/1/01).

121

# Bill Goes to War

**B**ill O'Reilly is perfectly consistent on one thing—flexing military muscle. O'Reilly's eagerness to back military action was not matched by eagerness to serve in Vietnam, however. After graduating from college, O'Reilly was a high school teacher in Florida and, according to a Fox spokesperson, received a deferment from serving. According to one newspaper account, O'Reilly "later volunteered to serve as a military policeman for a fort in Brooklyn but was not asked to serve" (*Ventura [Calif.] County Star*, 2/13/02).

Nonetheless, he has backed military action on a number of occasions and in language that is exceedingly brutal. While he flinched at Bill Moyers's calling him a warmonger, it's hard to think of a more appropriate term.

**This is a different world than it was in World War II, when the Geneva Convention was put into effect, that we're fighting a war on terror, and—biological, no problem. Nuclear, no problem. Civilians killed, no problem. My contention is you have to fight terror with terror. (11/8/01)**

**If NATO is not able to wear down this Milosevic in the next few weeks, I believe that we have to go in there and drop leaflets on Belgrade and other cities and say, "Listen, you**

**guys have got to move because we're now going to come in and we're going to just level your country. The whole infrastructure is going. (4/26/99)**

These "principles" also apply to military actions that O'Reilly wasn't able to cover as a journalist, like the bombing of Japanese cities at the end of World War II—actions O'Reilly wholeheartedly endorsed: "In World War II, we had to defeat the Japanese. It wasn't a crime!" When guest Ron Daniels of the Center for Constitutional Rights asked how many innocents had died, O'Reilly was unmoved: "There were no innocent people! They all supported their government" (1/31/03).

**The German people in Dresden and all those other cities, when they were bombed out—I'm not weeping for those people. (4/26/99)**

That position is somewhat different than some of his other statements:

**You can make all the excuses you want, but only barbarians attack women and children. (4/2/02)**

Then again, consistency is just not his strong suit:

**O'REILLY: If the Taliban government of Afghanistan does not cooperate, then we will damage that government with air power, probably. All right? We will blast them.**

**Sam Husseini (Institute for Public Accuracy): Who will you kill in the process?**

**O'REILLY: Doesn't make any difference. (9/13/01)**

## Insane vs. Illegal?

After September 11, O'Reilly seemed to argue that virtually any military action was justified. Any suggestions to the contrary were brushed off as either irrelevant or crazy:

> **Here's [Congressman] Ron Paul, a Republican from Texas. I'll read you his statement because we don't have a video on it. "There is compelling moral argument against the war in Iraq. Military force is justified only in self-defense; naked aggression is the province of dictators and rogue states. This is the danger of a new 'preemptive first-strike' doctrine."**

O'Reilly couldn't relate to Paul's argument at all. "The only military force is justified in self-defense. OK. So, basically, what Paul is saying that we have to get nuked here before we can stop the nukes. This is insane" (4/11/03).

What O'Reilly is calling "insane" is essentially the same legal doctrine that was used to prosecute Nazi war criminals at Nuremberg. As the International Court declared, "To initiate a war of aggression, therefore, is not only an international crime, it is the supreme international crime differing only from other war crimes in that it contains within itself the accumulated evil of the whole" (cited by Walter J. Rockler, former Nuremberg prosecutor, *Chicago Tribune*, 5/23/99). As the head of the American team at Nuremberg, Supreme Court Justice Robert Jackson argued that "launching a war of aggression is a crime and that no political or economic situation can justify it."

## Who Else Wants a Piece?

It's one thing to promote your country's drive to war. But O'Reilly takes it a step further, advocating new and unusual military adventures.

## CUBA

What is important is that Castro does no harm to the USA, because if he does, in this climate, the Bay of Pigs might have a very different sequel. (5/14/02)

## DRUG TRAFFICKING IN COLOMBIA? BOMB THEM!

How about air power like we did over in Yugoslavia? . . . You want to knock out these narco-traffickers, you've got to do it from the air. (2/22/01)

## WHEN STORIES OF CHINESE ESPIONAGE WERE BIG NEWS, O'REILLY SAW A LOOMING BATTLE

So let me put this to you viewers under the age of thirty. Do you think you could physically win a fight against the Chinese? Could you do what your fathers and grandfathers did, slug it out in hot jungles with men dying all around you? Could you stand there and fight while thousands of well-trained, fanatical Communist soldiers came at you? Could you do that? I believe that many Americans have gone soft, not only physically, but mentally, as well. The Chinese are dangerous, they pose a threat to us. They stole our technology and our government's lame response is embarrassing, to say the least. (5/24/99)

## WISHING WAR ON SOUTH KOREA

They elected a president who, you know, his agenda is not what the Bush administration's agenda is. They had two choices: a guy who supported the Bush administration and a guy who didn't. So look, I say we don't need South Korea. Why are we spending all the money over there anyway? Pull them [U.S. troops] out of there. . . .

Let the South Koreans do it themselves. . . . They got a lot of demonstrations and a lot of energy. Let them do it. See, I don't have any sympathy for them. In fact, I would say to the North Koreans, "Look, you can invade them, we don't care. Just knock down your nuclear, take them over." They deserve to be taken over. (1/2/03)

## Osama bin O'Reilly?

"The people of any country are ultimately responsible for the government they have. The Germans were responsible for Hitler. The Afghans are responsible for the Taliban. We should not target civilians. But if they don't rise up against this criminal government, they starve, period." (Bill O'Reilly, 9/17/01)

"We differentiate between the man, the woman, the child, and the old people. The man is a fighter, whether he carries arms or helps kill us by paying taxes and by gathering information. He is a fighter . . . Our enemy, the target if God gives Muslims the opportunity to do so—is every American male, whether he is directly fighting us or paying taxes." (Osama bin Laden, 1998 interview with Al Jazeera; portions re-aired on CBS, 9/26/01)

## FOOD AS A WEAPON IN NORTH KOREA

This strikes me—giving these people food, the North Koreans, at this juncture—the same thing as if we gave the Nazis food during World War II and the Japanese food during World War II. (1/6/03)

## O'REILLY NOT ONLY HAS ADVICE FOR WHEN TO GO TO WAR—HE'S ALSO GIVEN SOME THOUGHT AS TO HOW A JOURNALIST SHOULD COVER IT

If you're with troops and you're with the Americans, you've got to follow their rules. And if they say jump, you've got to jump. If they say don't report it, you can't report it. If they say off the record, this is off the record. . . . You're not part of the troops, but you've got to obey the orders. . . . If you're with a military unit and they give you an order, you obey it. Period. (4/1/03)

ED ASNER: Why didn't the United States go into Cambodia and save the million and a half Cambodians that were being slaughtered?

O'REILLY: Because of antiwar demonstrators. That's why. (9/26/02)

# O'Reilly's America

**I'm a big civil liberties guy. And I don't want people spying on me, but I also want sanity. I want sanity, not political correctness. (SPEECH AT HARVARD UNIVERSITY, AIRED 5/6/02.)**

From Guantánamo detainees to legal disputes in American courtrooms, it's hard to think of a media figure who has done more to support the Bush administration's post–September 11 restrictions on civil liberties than Bill O'Reilly. Attorney General John Ashcroft's memorable warning to dissenters, "Your tactics only aid terrorists, for they erode our national unity and diminish our resolve," bears a striking resemblance to O'Reilly's own thinking about dissidents, lawyers with unpopular clients, and international human rights groups: "I've pretty much had it with Amnesty International," he said on 5/29/02. Discussing the definition of treason in reference to the John Walker Lindh case, O'Reilly joked that it might also apply to "some of the peaceniks that are walking around, but that would be a little bit of a stretch here" (12/4/01).

O'Reilly's opinions on freedom of speech are not necessarily linked to any post-9/11 awakening. Some of his ideas were in place long before then. A self-described "big free speech guy," O'Reilly lays out bizarre

opinions on the subject. Explaining his support for Congressional action to ban flag burning, O'Reilly argued, "Freedom of speech does not allow a person to intentionally inflict pain on someone else. . . . Flag burning is disrespectful to Americans and seems to be an intentional infliction of emotional distress" (6/24/99). If O'Reilly really believed that the legal limits of free speech would be determined by "emotional distress," flag burning would be just the tip of the iceberg—many people are distressed by Bill O'Reilly every night.

O'Reilly took a similarly broad approach to limiting free speech rights when he railed against a VH1 cable show that profiled prison inmates who made music. "VH1 is making money on this program solely because these men committed crimes . . . If these men did not commit the crimes, they couldn't put them on, they couldn't have a program to sell. So therefore, I believe they're committing a criminal act" (12/2/02).

O'Reilly expanded the argument by claiming that free speech should be most available to those who can prove the "worth" of their words, and "I don't think VH1 can prove any worth to this." When a Fox legal analyst tried to explain that "You don't have to prove worth in order to speak in the public forum. That's what the First Amendment protects," O'Reilly countered that the show was "actions, not words."

Expressing political dissent is also an optional freedom for O'Reilly. Here's his take on civil disobedience: "Here's how I see it. I think every American has the obligation to obey the law, number one. That's their primary obligation. Obey the law. If you don't, you're un-American. If you break the law, you're un-American" (10/9/02). When O'Reilly's guest sug-

> **ON DEFENSE ATTORNEYS:**
> "They want to give their clients the best defense possible, and that means challenging the source of the information it gets against those clients. At a time of war, this cannot be allowed to happen. All suspected terrorists and those captured on foreign battlefields should be tried by the military, period" (2/11/03).

gested that "Martin Luther King, by that definition, was un-American," O'Reilly was hardly moved: "All right, you could stretch it. . . . There is always an asterisk, professor. You know, you guys in your ivory tower."

## The First Amendment Violates Bill O'Reilly's Rights

When a California appeals court ruled that the phrase "under God" in the Pledge of Allegiance was unconstitutional, O'Reilly was furious: "Say goodbye to the Pledge of Allegiance, at least for now" (6/26/02). O'Reilly opened his show the next night with the warning, "God under siege in America." The decision was an "insult to the Constitution," a "violation of every American, every American who sees this country in a historical context."

That context, as O'Reilly sees it, is obvious to anyone but that "pinhead judge" in California: God has influenced America right from the start, "the spirit is driven by the Founding Fathers, as you know, they had chaplains, the Creator, and all of that thing. . . . If the Founding Fathers didn't want any mention of God, they would have said it." In fact, at the Constitutional Convention, a proposal by Ben Franklin to open sessions with prayer and to hire a chaplain was dismissed without a vote. "The convention, except three or four persons, thought prayers unnecessary!" a shocked Franklin wrote in his notes (H. W. Brands, *The First American: The Life and Times of Benjamin Franklin*, Doubleday, 2000).

The Ninth Circuit decision found that the phrase "under God" unconstitutionally endorsed a religious doctrine. For O'Reilly, that's a threshold that's rarely met: When an elementary school puts up a sign that says "God Bless America," according to O'Reilly, that "doesn't endorse a religion. It doesn't encourage anybody to be spiritual. It makes a statement that says 'God Bless America.' That's all it does" (10/10/01).

O'Reilly even goes so far as to assert that the majority has a right to put its sacred texts on display in government offices. When the governor of Indiana was blocked from posting the Ten Commandments on state property, O'Reilly complained that the Commandments are "a historical document written, pardon the pun, in stone. They establish methods of behavior for those interested in having a life based upon the respect of others and the higher power, spirituality. So why are the courts intruding on history? Why do I not have the right as an American to read in a government office the basic tenets that our civil laws are based on? Somebody is violating my rights here" (2/25/02).

For O'Reilly, such unpleasant court decisions are supremely personal, as he explained to one guest: "It is offensive to me and a million of Americans, that we can't mention the word 'God' without people like you and the ACLU saying, 'You don't have the right, Bill O'Reilly, as an American, to mention a three-letter word. No matter what the context is, you don't have the right to do that.' That's outrageous" (10/10/01).

O'Reilly isn't *always* outraged when religious expression is restricted, however. As he explained to a Muslim police officer in Chicago who wanted to wear a head scarf under her regulation-issued hat, "But deputy, I do have a little bit of a problem with this, as far as separation of church and state is concerned. We're a secular society. You work for a state. And religion is supposed to be kept out of the public arena. Yet you are a law enforcement official representing the state of Illinois. Do you see the problem there?" (7/11/02)

## O'Reilly's Courts

In O'Reilly's world, the rights of defendants pale in comparison to the rights of the prosecution. He's passionate about the difficulties involved in locking people up. After a guilty verdict in one case he was following wasn't reached quickly enough, O'Reilly suggested: "We might want to go from reasonable doubt to preponderance of evidence as a basis of conviction" (8/21/02).

When all else fails, O'Reilly argues that law should be made to fit the crime. Discussing his disappointment with the prosecution of Global Crossing CEO Gary Winnick, O'Reilly offered this insight to one of his guests: "What you say is probably correct—he didn't break any laws. Although if I were the Justice Department, I'd find a law, OK?" (3/7/02)

O'Reilly was enraged by the actions of one particular defense attorney, John Pozza, who had successfully defended a client who then went on to kill a young girl. O'Reilly played a clip of CNN's *Larry King Live* in which Pozza said, "A guilty man did not go free. A jury came back and acquitted Mr. Avila." O'Reilly's response: "There it is. In the world that counselor Pozza lives in, there is no guilt if the jury doesn't convict" (7/30/02). Yes, innocent until proven guilty is the basis of our legal system, actually.

> **The problem is, we're not fighting this war on terror effectively enough because we're hung up on the rights issue. (6/12/02)**

## PATRIOT Act

Civil libertarians have raised an outcry over the drastic changes in government authority written into the USA PATRIOT Act of 2001. But O'Reilly, despite his professed concern for civil rights, could hardly contain his disdain in an interview with Cambridge, Massachusetts, councilmember Brian Murphy, after the city council voted to criticize the civil liberties restrictions in the post–September 11 bill. "If I were a terrorist, you know where I'd live?" O'Reilly told his guest. "On Mass Ave. in Cambridge. That's where I would go, because you guys are going to protect me" (7/1/02).

O'Reilly was unconvinced when Murphy explained his opposition to "sneak and peek" searches, where authorities can conduct a search without showing a warrant until after the search is completed. O'Reilly interrupted Murphy's explanation of the law to assert that "they have to show you the warrant, and you have a certain right to look at that warrant." Not under the PATRIOT Act—that was Murphy's point.

Requiring libraries or bookstores to turn over their records to the FBI was no big deal to O'Reilly, since such searches are "predicated upon a crime or a terrorist act." He likened reading a suspicious book to "hiding cocaine in the Boston Public Library or in any bookstore in Boston or Cambridge. . . . It's the same thing." But under Section 215 of the USA PATRIOT Act, reading a book is not the same thing as selling cocaine: the FBI can much more easily investigate your reading habits, simply by asserting that the search is part of an investigation "to protect against international terrorism or clandestine intelligence activities." And "the FBI need not suspect the person whose records are being sought of any wrongdoing," notes Nancy Chang in her book *Silencing Political Dissent* (Seven Stories, 2002).

> **Evil does exist in this world. In the United States, it has hidden behind the First Amendment, and been sheltered by the numbing narrowness of politically correct thought.**
> **(column, 12/1/01)**

Nonetheless, O'Reilly saw no reason to question the law. "We tried to find out anybody, any American citizen who had filed a lawsuit or had gone public with any kind of an abuse by the part of the FBI or federal authorities on their rights. We can't find any. So it looks to me like you're hysterical in Cambridge . . . and number two, that you may be seditious, that you may be undermining this government."

"Seditious" or not, it's not difficult to find people who are concerned about the USA PATRIOT Act, especially Section 215. But one would have to be familiar with the actual law to understand just how difficult it can be to go public with such concerns. As the *San Francisco Chronicle* explained, "Librarians and booksellers are prohibited, under threat of prosecution, from revealing an FBI visit to anyone, including the patron whose records were seized" (6/23/02).

134

## "Hiding Behind the Constitution"

Lawyers who defend unpopular clients come in for special abuse on *The O'Reilly Factor*.

> **The truth is that American lawyers can pick and choose whom they want to represent, and if their tactics put the public in jeopardy, as these cases do, those lawyers are responsible.... You can hide behind the Constitution all day long, but endangering the lives of Americans is a crime in itself, no matter what venue you may be in. (6/17/02)**

This hostility toward lawyers who represent terrorism suspects sometimes leads O'Reilly to stretch the facts. He claimed that the lawyers for accused shoe-bomber Richard Reid "have asked for the security plans for all U.S. airports, thereby putting me and my family in jeopardy" (6/17/02). Reid's attorney, Owen Walker, told FAIR that O'Reilly's assertion was "hogwash," that the defense has asked for no such thing. O'Reilly may be confusing the Reid case with another post–September 11 legal matter: lawyers for some of the families of those killed "have been seeking records involving airline security and other information that could expose the vulnerabilities or failures of the airlines, airports, and government agencies," according to the *New York Times* (7/13/02). Perhaps O'Reilly should be directing his anger at widows and orphans instead.

Lawyers who choose to defend terror suspects such as Richard Reid don't have to just worry about answering to Bill O'Reilly. On October 31, 2001, Attorney General John Ashcroft declared that he would allow his department to eavesdrop on conversations between federal prisoners and their lawyers. O'Reilly rejected the idea that this was an infringement on the Sixth Amendment right to effective counsel: "The attorney

general was only speaking about noncitizens, not citizens of the United States," he said, adding that "the Constitution was written for citizens of the United States. . . . Are you going to tell me that all noncitizens in the world should have the same rights as Americans when they enter this country?" (1/10/02)

There are two problems with O'Reilly's defense of Ashcroft: First, the rule makes no mention of nationality, applying to citizens and noncitizens alike; and second, it is well established that the right to effective counsel is available even to noncitizens who are to be tried in the U.S. justice system. But the principle of legal protection for noncitizens is something O'Reilly simply refuses to believe: "Tell me where in the Constitution it says that foreigners are to be given the same rights as U.S. citizens. Can you point that out to me, please?" O'Reilly asked one guest. As he reads it, "in the preamble of the Constitution it says, 'We the People of the United States of America [sic].' Not Pakistan, not Yemen." When another guest explained that the "Supreme Court of the United States stated just two terms ago that if you're here legally or illegally, you're entitled to due process of law," O'Reilly's response was blunt: "That's insane" (2/15/02).

But it's not just noncitizens who should have some of their rights waived, in O'Reilly's judgment. Arguing that "dirty bomb" suspect (and U.S. citizen) Jose Padilla shouldn't be allowed a trial in civil court because his alleged crimes occurred overseas, "You know as well as I do that constitutional guarantees, all right, end when you leave this country. You don't have any constitutional guarantee of anything once you go on foreign soil" (1/9/03).

## Misrule of Law

O'Reilly has often derided the Geneva Convention as inapplicable to fighting a "war on terror," but it's not clear he understands what the

Geneva Convention says. Defending the treatment of prisoners at Guantánamo Bay, he asserted that "The Geneva Convention doesn't say you have to house prisoners of war the same way you would house your own prisoners" (1/21/02). In fact, the convention requires countries' POW housing to match the quality of their *barracks*, not their prisons (Part III, Section II, Chapter 2, Article 25): "Prisoners of war shall be quartered under conditions as favorable as those for the forces of the Detaining Power who are billeted in the same area."

O'Reilly produces other creative legal citations. Bush's war on terror would be enhanced if he would "allow federal authorities to incarcerate illegals in this country and deport them under the War Powers Act" (6/7/02). The War Powers Act requires the president to have Congressional approval to keep troops in battle—it doesn't say anything about rounding up or deporting anyone.

That's not O'Reilly's only confusing War Powers citation, though. He defended the administration's use of military tribunals "under the War Powers Act, even though—War Powers applies even in undeclared war, as Vietnam. The president has a right to intern, as the Japanese were in World War II" (12/5/01). The War Powers Act was enacted in 1973, so it hardly relates to the World War II internments, which were carried out under a presidential executive order.

## "A Subversive Woman"

O'Reilly's contempt for international law and lawyers who defend "repugnant" suspects also extends to judges who defend constitutional rights. On April 30, 2002, New York District Court Judge Shira Scheindlin dismissed perjury charges against Osama Awadallah, a Jordanian student acquainted with two of the September 11 hijackers. Awadallah, like dozens of others arrested after the World Trade Center attacks, had been detained as a material witness in a grand jury investigation.

Scheindlin ruled that jailing people simply to ensure that they testify before a grand jury was unconstitutional.

O'Reilly called Scheindlin a "subversive woman" who was "releasing a man that could be a terrorist" and issued a call "for the House Judiciary Committee to seek the authority from the entire House to begin an impeachment inquiry into the judge" (6/6/02). He concluded that "Scheindlin has a long antigovernment record. Her main duty is to protect Americans from harm, yet she allows a man who is associated with two terrorist killers to walk free, unsupervised. All of us should contact our congressperson immediately."

The next night, O'Reilly responded to a critical letter from a viewer by summing up his position: "Just want to have an investigation into this. I'm not saying remove her yet" (6/7/02). Viewers who paid attention the previous day, though, might remember O'Reilly's message differently: "Judge Scheindlin has to go" (6/6/02).

On other occasions, though, O'Reilly stands up for his anticonstitutional beliefs. In an argument about the use of military tribunals, Fox legal analyst Andrew Napolitano put this question to him: "Do you want to take away human liberty that the Constitution guarantees to all persons because of the clothing a person wears, because of where they happen to be born, because of what their nationality is?" (12/5/01)

O'Reilly's response? "Yes, I do."

# Case Study—Iraq

**We hope you depend on us for the truth, because we're going to report the situation in Iraq without an agenda or any ideological prejudice.** (1/17/03)

If there's one issue that provides a showcase for all the worst qualities of Bill O'Reilly's journalism, it's his reporting and commentary on the war with Iraq. Prior to the September 11 attacks, O'Reilly had no particular interest in the threat Iraq posed to the world: "You know, I don't take Saddam Hussein all that seriously anymore as far as a world threat. Maybe I'm wrong and naive here. Should we be very frightened of this guy?" (2/16/01) If the Bill O'Reilly of today were to meet the Bill O'Reilly of 2001, he'd denounce him as an appeaser, a coward, or much worse. As he fumed to one guest skeptical of war with Iraq, the menace that is Saddam Hussein has been well established: "We have gone through this and through this and through this for more than a decade with this man"(1/14/03).

The Bush administration's restless determination to mount a massive ground invasion of Iraq was matched by O'Reilly's unwavering support for their effort. O'Reilly told viewers that his show was the place to get "the best coverage of Iraq" (2/14/03), but it actually offered a parade of logical inconsistencies and bungled facts.

139

On the question of Iraq's banned weapons—the core rationale for going to war—O'Reilly displayed a remarkable flexibility:

> **I can't, in good conscience, tell the American people that I know for sure that he has smallpox or anthrax or he's got nuclear or chemical and that he is ready to use that. I cannot say that as a journalist or an American. (12/6/02)**

But soon O'Reilly was able to shift his rhetoric:

> **According to the UN, he's got anthrax, VX gas, ricin, and on and on. (2/17/03)**

> **This guy we know has anthrax and VX and all this stuff. (2/26/03)**

O'Reilly even conjured up a link between the 2001 anthrax mailings and Iraq, telling Congressman Pete DeFazio (Democrat, Oregon), a critic of the war, "You're going to put all of us at risk because you don't think he's going to do it . . . He might have been responsible for the anthrax letter" (2/5/03).

To make matters more confusing, during an appearance on ABC's *Good Morning America* on March 18, 2003, O'Reilly was back to his original position: "Here's the bottom line on this for every American and everybody in the world: Nobody knows for sure, all right? We don't know what he has. We think he has eighty-five hundred liters of anthrax. But let's see."

## Finding a Reason

Throughout the debate that preceded the war, O'Reilly was on the hunt for any pretext that might justify an invasion. "We basically feel that he is a danger to our oil supply there," he explained to one guest (1/14/03). As diplomacy and weapons inspections were underway, O'Reilly grew increasingly frustrated with the pace of events. Critical press coverage of Bush's Iraq policy in the foreign media was "an orchestrated campaign to denigrate the Bush administration and our attempt to remove a ferocious dictator" (1/21/03).

"'Talking Points' is distressed to see some American reporters doing sympathetic pieces about the Iraqi people" (1/24/03). Yes, those Iraqi people—the ones whose liberation was the main justification offered by war supporters, at least after the fact. Before the war, O'Reilly certainly placed little emphasis on that rationale: "What they don't mention is that after the Gulf War in 1991 the Iraqi people had the opportunity to overthrow this terrible dictator. They did not. Now the American people must provide billions of tax dollars in order to remove him. Now, I don't know about you, but I don't have a lot of sympathy for the Iraqi people" (1/24/02).

## The Reason Hunt

O'Reilly presented a more palatable justification for war in Iraq's response to weapons inspections—or so he thought. "Saddam Hussein can kiss his ass goodbye," O'Reilly gloated on his January 9, 2003, broadcast. "Chief UN weapons inspector Hans Blix told the United Nations Security Council today that Saddam will not let inspectors interview Iraqi scientists."

But that never happened. As the *Los Angeles Times* reported, "Referring to efforts to speak to Iraqi scientists, Blix told reporters after the meeting that a lot of interviews have been carried out and a lot of information has been gathered when inspectors visit installations" (1/10/03). (Blix did raise questions at that briefing about the completeness of the list of scientists provided by Iraq.)

Another rationale O'Reilly offered for going to war with Iraq was September 11, though no evidence of an Iraq–al Qaeda link had emerged in the year and a half since the attacks.

When he asked Representative Diane Watson (Democrat, California) if she would have pursued diplomacy instead of war with Japan or Hitler, and she reminded him that the Japanese had "struck Pearl Harbor," O'Reilly replied, "And we got wiped out at the World Trade Center and the Pentagon" (10/10/02).

O'Reilly had suggested an Iraq link to September 11 as early as September 14, 2001: "Saddam Hussein . . . I believe is involved with this World Trade Center and Pentagon bombing. I believe that you're going to find out that money from Iraq flowed in and helped this happen."

## "Read the Treaty"

O'Reilly also presented the case for war in legal terms. "Number one, he [Saddam Hussein] has violated the Gulf War surrender terms," O'Reilly explained (9/10/02). "Just that alone means the USA has a right to oust him." As he argued to Representative Sheila Jackson Lee (Democrat, Texas), "We do have the moral authority to remove him because he violated the Gulf War treaty. Surely you understand that. . . . We can go in and morally remove him. . . . Read the treaty, congresswoman. . . . If he violates his terms, we can then resume hostilities" (10/10/02).

The Gulf War ended with a permanent cease-fire when Iraq formally accepted UN Security Council Resolution 686 in March 1991 (*Washington Post*, 3/4/91). That resolution required Iraq to withdraw from Kuwait, pay reparations for the damage caused there, and grant access to POWs. Another resolution, 687, was adopted by the Security Council in April 1991 and declared that "a formal cease-fire is effective between Iraq and Kuwait and the Member States cooperating with Kuwait." Iraq accepted this as the final cease-fire terms on April 7, 1991 (*New York Times*, 4/8/03).

Though this second resolution did require significant Iraqi disarmament, it did not give a blank check to the United States or any other

nation to resume war against Iraq. As Columbia University law professor Michael C. Dorf pointed out, Resolution 687 "stated the Security Council's intention 'to take as appropriate all necessary measures' to guarantee the inviolability of the Iraq-Kuwait border," while on the issue of disarmament, the Security Council resolved "to remain seized of the matter and to take such further steps as may be required for the implementation of the present resolution and to secure peace and security in the area" (www.findlaw.com, 3/19/03). Note that Resolution 687 authorized the Security Council, *and not individual states*, to take any needed actions.

But these facts don't seem to matter: when former weapons inspector Scott Ritter challenged O'Reilly's creative legal interpretation, O'Reilly's response was a shrug. "All right, you disagree, fine. . . . You can disagree, we'll let the audience decide" (9/12/02).

## Creeping Streisandism

Diplomatic niceties are seldom the order of the day on *The O'Reilly Factor* —especially when people aren't there to defend their positions. Actor Sean Penn, who visited Baghdad prior to the bombing, "is an idiot," according to O'Reilly (1/2/03). "He doesn't know anything. He has no frame of reference. He has no idea where he is, and he was allowed to be used by Saddam Hussein."

O'Reilly had a whole list of Iraq-related enemies: "France, Britain [sic], Barbra Streisand, and Congressman Jim McDermott. . . . Saddam Hussein must be very happy with all those guys," he asserted, explaining that McDermott "showed up last night on Phil Donahue's program to justify his giving aid and comfort to Saddam while he was in Baghdad" (10/3/02).

Even this limited tolerance for dissent evaporated as war approached: "Once the war against Saddam begins, we expect every American to

support our military, and if they can't do that, to shut up. Americans, and indeed our allies, who actively work against our military once the war is underway will be considered enemies of the state by me. Just fair warning to you, Barbra Streisand, and others who see the world as you do" (2/26/03).

Miles Solay of Not In Our Name appeared on O'Reilly's show to discuss the group's antiwar advertisement in the *New York Times*, which O'Reilly dubbed a "bit of un-American propaganda" as "the ad states that America has no moral right to remove terrorists, because we ourselves are terrorists. This is dishonest, disgusting, and un-American, period" (1/27/03). The fact that the ad really said no such thing did not impress O'Reilly, who added, "I didn't hear a word from you, Miles, or any of your organization, when President Clinton initiated the regime change in Yugoslavia. You didn't say a word about it. And none of these pinheads would have signed it, because they like Clinton." O'Reilly made the same charge against *The Progressive*'s Matt Rothschild, who indeed did criticize the bombing of Serbia, as did some of the "pinheads" who signed Not In Our Name's ad. The group itself was founded in March 2002, making it somewhat difficult for them to criticize a bombing in 1999.

O'Reilly also claimed that the ad was "offensive to the families of lost people," a reference to the victims of the September 11 attacks. When Solay pointed out that some September 11 families had signed the petition, O'Reilly waved him off: "Nobody signed this from September 11." When Solay gave him the name of one family member, O'Reilly was determined: "We'll get that guy Jeremy Glick on tomorrow if that's the case," adding somewhat defensively, "I'm not sure it is the case."

Unfortunately, O'Reilly did carry through on his pledge to quiz Glick, whose father died at the World Trade Center. O'Reilly was more combative than usual, telling Glick that "I don't think your father would be approving of this," and "I hope your mother is not watching this" (2/4/03). When Glick tried to explain his reasons for not supporting the

bombing of Afghanistan ("Why would I want to brutalize and further punish the people in Afghanistan?"), O'Reilly screamed that they were the ones "who killed your father!" The disgraceful exchange concluded with O'Reilly saying, "Cut his mic. I'm not going to dress you down anymore, out of respect for your father." According to a Not In Our Name press release following the show, O'Reilly threatened Glick after the cameras were off: "Get out, get out of my studio before I tear you to fucking pieces!" (2/6/03)

At one point O'Reilly pulled back. "I made a mistake yesterday. Can you believe it?" he began one program (2/27/03). "I was wrong when I said that Americans who continue demonstrating against the war once the shooting begins are being un-American. I'm taking that back." As O'Reilly explained, "People who lawfully dissent should never be labeled 'un-American.' Instead, I will call those who publicly criticize our country in a time of military crisis, which this is, 'bad Americans.'"

Don't think for a minute that O'Reilly had gone soft, though. During a discussion about civil disobedience as a means of war protest, O'Reilly explained that "any American who commits civil disobedience in this time of war and terror is putting other Americans in danger" (3/19/03). O'Reilly added that "It is morally wrong for them to do it. They should be condemned by Americans and shunned," and that punishment should be severe: "I'll tell you what, if I were a prosecutor, I'd charge them with multiple felonies. I'd make their life a living hell." He even figured an appropriate dollar amount for those arrested for civil disobedience: "Give them a warning. If they don't leave, then arrest them and fine them $100,000" (3/31/03).

## Blank You!

O'Reilly also saved some venom for countries that were not behind the war. "Canada shows its true colors," O'Reilly began one broadcast,

directing his fire towards Prime Minister Jean Chretien. "The prime minister is against removing Saddam Hussein without a worldwide mandate, which will never happen because many nations hate the U.S. and will do anything to hurt us. . . . If Jean Chretien doesn't understand that, no one can help him. It is up to the good citizens of Canada to give him the boot" (9/12/02). O'Reilly finished off by giving an e-mail address for the Canadian embassy, so Americans could tell the "prime minister that we think his opinions and attitudes are misguided."

The treatment of Canada seemed downright civil compared to O'Reilly's attitude toward Germany. "Well, with all due respect, blank you, Mr. Chancellor," was O'Reilly's message to German Chancellor Gerhard Schroeder (8/6/02). An earlier O'Reilly column was more broad, but the message was just as coarse: "The entire European Union is a problem in the war on terror, not just Deutschland. The EU has told the Bush administration that it has a 'problem' with trying captured terrorists in front of military tribunals. Well, pardon me, EU, but *blank* you" (www.worldnetdaily.com, 6/13/02).

## "Don't Buy French Stuff!"

O'Reilly's next step was a boycott of French products. The rationale was that an Internet poll at www.billoreilly.com showed that his readers overwhelmingly supported an economic boycott of most French imports. "Now, we are all soldiers in the war against terror here in America, and our weapon is our wallet. If France does, indeed, veto a new UN resolution, I will support a boycott of their products, and even if it doesn't come to that, I myself will think long and hard before I buy anything made in France."

O'Reilly soldiered on even after the UN resolution authorizing force was pulled off the table by the United States. All that was left was to count the votes: "So far, almost thirty thousand people have weighed in.

Ninety-three percent say they support a boycott" (3/13/03). On March 17, O'Reilly was reporting that "almost eighty thousand people took part in a billoreilly.com poll last week from all over the world that asked the question: Should Americans boycott French products? An astounding 95 percent said yes. The largest plurality we've ever seen. Just 4 percent said no."

When French journalist Phillipe Coste had the temerity to suggest that maybe a poll on Bill O'Reilly's website might not accurately represent public opinion in America, O'Reilly wasn't having it: "With all due respect, Mr. Coste, you're wrong. I mean, I do a radio program for two hours every single day with 360 radio stations from coast to coast, and 90 percent of my callers just are so furious" (3/17/03).

Besides his somewhat absurd claim that there were "millions of Americans refusing to buy French products" based on the results of his poll, there was also an ironic twist to the whole episode. Months earlier, O'Reilly had commissioned a scientific poll to determine whether a Planned Parenthood slogan was offensive to Americans. On a CNN program a few days later, viewers were encouraged to vote on CNN's website about the controversy.

O'Reilly was furious at this: "CNN picks up the story after our reporting and does what they call a Quickvote. That's a website–driven survey of viewers who watch CNN." One lesson from this, according to O'Reilly, was that "CNN will feature on-air surveys that really have no validity at all." O'Reilly's conclusion: "'Talking Points' believes that featuring Internet polls as news is cheap and misleading." Unless, of course, it's a Bill O'Reilly Internet poll.

## "Flatten Baghdad"

Once the war began, O'Reilly was immediately frustrated by two things: "negative" media coverage that portrayed the invasion as anything less

than a smashing success, and the "politically correct" war being conducted by the United States and its allies. The politically incorrect strategy O'Reilly called for was the complete destruction of Baghdad, a city of 4.5 million residents:

> There is a school of thought that says we should have given the citizens of Baghdad forty-eight hours to "get out of Dodge" by dropping leaflets and going with the AM radios and all that. Forty-eight hours, you've got to get out of there, and flatten the place. Then the war would be over. We could have done that in two days. . . . You flatten Baghdad, you flatten all the troops, we know where they go, there's nowhere to hide in the desert. We know where everybody's moving. And you know as well as I do, this war could have been over in two days. . . . It's just frustrating for everybody to know that we have been fighting this war with one hand behind our back. (3/26/03)

And let there be no doubt about where the real responsibility for the safety of the Iraqi people lies: "Now after we know that the final battle is going to come to Baghdad, that the people who remain in Baghdad, the civilians, bear some kind of responsibility for their own safety. Am I wrong?" O'Reilly's guests that night were in agreement.

# "Sheer O'Reillyness"

It's very likely Bill O'Reilly really does believe that California judges he disagrees with are all "appointed by liberal politicians," or that Hillary Clinton makes a bad choice for the Senate because she's never been to Rochester. He probably does think that France "opposed bombing Serbia," or that "the average American pays twice as much federal tax now as it did in 1985 under President Reagan." And it's quite likely that O'Reilly is of the opinion that you "never hear a pro-life person on NPR. You never hear an anti–global warming person on NPR." None of these things are true, though. But O'Reilly's confidence in the righteousness of his pronouncements makes his words seem believable. After finding out, while writing a profile of him, that statements O'Reilly had made about another media outlet were inaccurate, one journalist chalked up her failure to check his claims to having been "mesmerized by O'Reilly's sheer O'Reillyness" (7/9/03).

She's not alone. According to one newspaper profile, O'Reilly is a media force to be reckoned with: "Fox News airs ten *Factor* repeats a week, his radio show reaches about 15 million people, and several million more have read his newspaper column. And his reach keeps expanding" (*Newark Star-Ledger*, 5/11/03).

O'Reilly clearly has an appeal (and maybe even an "O'Reillyness"). This book doesn't seek to explain his popularity. Nor is the point to crit-

icize O'Reilly's politics; O'Reilly makes them an issue only by denying that he's a conservative.

The deceptive spin, garbled facts, and twisted logic outlined in this book aren't intended to pass for a comprehensive look at O'Reilly's record. But there's no shortage of material. Take O'Reilly's pledge on the claims about Iraq and weapons of mass destruction: "If the Americans go in and overthrow Saddam Hussein and it's clean, he has nothing, I will apologize to the nation, and I will not trust the Bush Administration again, all right?" (ABC, 3/18/03). That might suggest that O'Reilly would be leading the criticism of the Bush administration for exaggerating the evidence against Iraq. O'Reilly said it himself: "If Bush lied—if he lied— I'll be the first one to hang him, OK?" (7/7/03). But it's hardly a surprise that O'Reilly was, on that particular night, fixated on "hanging" Bush's critics. When he learned that columnist William Pfaff wrote in the *New York Times*–owned *International Herald Tribune* about the "culture of lies that prevails in the Bush administration," O'Reilly was seething: "What the heck is this guy doing and why is the *New York Times* letting him do it?" He fumed that "the *New York Times* and the *International Herald Tribune* should be ashamed of themselves for putting out this propaganda, not demanding their columnists back it up with some kind of data." O'Reilly's viewers were likely unaware that Pfaff's claims were indeed "backed up" in his column by a list of the White House's deceptions and misstatements. O'Reilly had just spent an entire segment claiming the opposite. Just another night in the "no-spin zone."

O'Reilly's self-confidence and confrontational style shouldn't disarm media critics—it should inspire more scrutiny. That's especially true when you consider that other news outlets, particularly on cable TV, might be trying to steal a page from O'Reilly's playbook. MSNBC, for example, hired Republican former Republican Congressman Joe Scarborough to host a a nightly show. He once said that "people around here call me 'Little O'Reilly.'" The insinuation is that something about *The*

*O'Reilly Factor*—whether it's the politics, the anger, or the combative style—will be imitated, if MSNBC management gets its way. In fact, Scarborough's commentary at the top of his show, called "The Real Deal," is nearly a carbon copy of O'Reilly's "Talking Points Memo." While it might get better ratings to imitate O'Reilly—the true measure of success, according to the dictates of cable news—it probably won't be good journalism. Or journalism at all, for that matter.

Every night, Bill O'Reilly closes his show the same way. He looks into the camera, points his pen at the audience, and grins: "And remember— the spin stops here." But in reality, that's where it starts.

151

# Acknowledgments

**S**pecial thanks to the entire staff at Seven Stories Press for their hard work and enthusiasm. This book would have been impossible without the assistance of my FAIR colleagues, past and present: Seth Ackerman, Rachel Coen, Jeff Cohen, Sanford Hohauser, Janine Jackson, Jim Naureckas, Steve Rendall and Deborah Thomas. I am grateful for your inspiration and guidance.

A number of FAIR's underappreciated interns provided invaluable assistance, trudging through transcripts and digging up quotes: Stephen Silver, Maxine Wu, Matt Dineen and Gwyneth Nowack-Greene.

Other writers, researchers and activists also shared their time and expertise: Dean Baker, Rob Boston, Michael Eisenmenger, H. Bruce Franklin, Tom Gorman, Eliot Katz, Andrew Lee, Mike Males, Harold Pollack, Bob Somerby and Chris Toensing. I am honored that Bob McChesney graciously agreed to write the foreword to this book. His insight and analysis are invaluable to the media democracy movement, and it is always a pleasure to be associated with him.

A special thank you (and possibly an apology) to my wife, who tolerated countless hours of *The O'Reilly Factor* in our home. Her patience was a blessing.

# Index

*The No Spin Zone* (book), 29–30
Not In Our Name, 144–145
Novak, Robert, 88
Nuclear Energy Institute (NEI), 101
nuclear power/energy, 101
nuclear readiness, 27
O'Donnell, Rosie, 22
*On the Media* (NPR radio show), 89, 115
*Orange County Register,* 114–115
O'Reilly, Bill
    on Allen Ginsberg, 36
    background of, 105, 119–121
    *Boston Globe* on, 34
    boycotts and, 30–31, 33, 60–61, 110–112, 130, 146–147
    and Bush, fondness for, 24, 36–38
    on campaign finance reform, 36
    Congressional aspirations of, 32
    conservatism of, 14, 18, 20
    on the Constitution, 53–54, 67–68, 108, 131, 135–136
    contradicting himself, 105–106
    on dissention, 130–131, 144–145
    on the Florida recount, 16, 37
    on homosexuality, 36, 43–45, 61–62
    on immigration, 79, 82, 99–100, 114

    on *Inside Edition,* 14–15
    Jesse Jackson, obsession with, 21, 26, 45–46
    on killing civilians, 108, 148
    and the No-Spin Zone, 11–12, 23–24
    and the O'Reilly "brand," 12
    paranoia of, 113–118
    popularity of, 11, 149–150
    racism of, 40–41, 45–49, 91, 102–103
    on religion, 131–132
    and the Republican Party, 31–32
    and the term "pinheads," 12, 144
    on war, 117–118, 123–128
*The O'Reilly Factor,* 8–9, 11, 14, 89, 97, 113–114, 120, 135, 143
*The O'Reilly Report,* 14
Padilla, Jose, 136
Parton, Dolly, 44
Passacantando, John, 13, 101
PATRIOT Act, 133–134
Paul, Ron, 125
Payton, Melissa, 93
Penn, Sean, 143
Pepsi-Cola, 30–31, 111–112
Pesca, Mike, 115
Pew Research Center, 89
Pfaff, William, 150
*Pittsburgh Post-Gazette,* 111
*Playboy,* 44
Pledge of Allegiance, 53–54, 131
police brutality, 69, 83

Pozza, John, 133
*The Progressive,* 144
Quayle, Dan, 94
Qutami, Leila, 64
racist remarks, 40–41, 45–49, 91, 102–103
Ramsey, JonBenet, 65
Rangel, Charles, 46
Rath, Arun, 115
Reagan, Ronald, 29
Reich, Robert, 34, 107
Reid, Richard, 135
religion, 28, 53–55, 105, 131–132
Reno, Janet, 16, 58
Reyes, Silvestre, 79–80
Rich, Marc, 40, 59
Richards, Ann, 38
Ritter, Scott, 23, 143
Robbins, Tim, 15
Rockler, Walter J., 125
Rosenberg, Howard, 14
Roth, Kenneth, 13
Rothschild, Matt, 144
Rumsfeld, Donald, 82
Russert, Tim, 89
Safire, William, 114
*San Francisco Chronicle,* 134
Santorum, Rick, 40
Sarandon, Susan, 15
Scarborough, Joe, 150–151
Scheiber, Noam, 120
Scheindlin, Shira, 137–138
Schlessinger, Laura, 61, 109
Schroeder, Gerhard, 146
secularism, 27
Sell, Michael Anthony, 116